SOME WORDS ABOUT
THE ANXIOUS HEARTS GUIDE

"As a relationship coach, I am well-aware of the overwhelming amount of existing literature on attachment, intimacy, communication, codependency, trauma, shame, and many other vital aspects of healing and emotional intelligence. Their volume alone makes them virtually inaccessible. I am equally aware that knowledge alone, though necessary, is woefully inadequate to transform the way you love.

In The Anxious Hearts Guide, Rikki Cloos gathers all of the relevant information, presents it with piercing clarity, and lays out specific, actionable steps to apply these concepts in your life. The book reads like a conversation with a best friend who always has the answers to your questions and advice you know you should take. It is chock-full of helpful resources and insights – truly a guide in every sense of the word."

- Adam Murauskas, FixYourPicker.com

"I have watched Rikki move from anxious to almost entirely secure in the short span of time that I've known her, just through her own deep self-reflection, dedication to learning, and grit to persevere. She has a remarkable gift to articulate that process to others in ways they can understand and implement right away, and I have no doubt that she is helping thousands of people heal their attachment wounds and salvage troubled relationships."

- @TheLovingAvoidant

"The Anxious Hearts Guide is a supportive and insightful resource for anyone who wants to understand the dynamics of anxious attachment style. In naming "anxious hearts," Rikki Cloos gives a name for a community of people who may have been previously misunderstood or misunderstood themselves in relationships. For someone who identifies as an "anxious heart," this guide offers everything about anxious attachment style in an easy-to-read format with real life strategies to help build a more secure attachment. It's a must read if you're an anxious heart or if you're in love with one.

- Bronwyn Heiss, LMHC, LMFT, Individual and Couples Therapist, fellow recovering anxious heart, working with anxious hearts and their partners

"This thing called life can be hard sometimes and it's ok to need help with it. 'The Anxious Hearts Guide' is exactly that, a helping hand for anyone struggling with attachment issues, especially the anxiously attached. Reading it feels a lot like having a personal coach, giving you background theory and laying the groundwork for your healing journey."

- Reader Marcel Span, The Netherlands

"I think the book is phenomenal.
I cried when I read one part because it made me see why I do what I do and woke me up to the reality of the situation.
I've read 60 pages in one sitting."

- Reader K., New York

"I'm not even 50 pages in but I have to tell you
that I've been working on my anxious attachment for a few years now
and have done a LOT of therapy, reading, and introspection
but your book is blowing me away!
I'm really glad you wrote it."

- Reader J., Pittsburgh, PA

"I haven't read a book cover to cover in less than 24 hours in a really long time. Nearly every single page resonated with me. For the first time in nearly 6 months I feel seen and it's amazing. The structure, the hope, the homework, the nonjudgmental, loving tone all felt like I have a new friend who sees me for who I am and wants to encourage me on my journey.

If there was one concept that resonated deeply at this point in my journey it's the idea that secure people feel "boring." Admittedly, I'm one of those "spark" and "passion" people. As I reflect back on past exes I can see how the secure ones are the ones who wanted to love me but I was bored. I didn't need to do anything to earn their affection and I simply didn't feel like I deserved it. So I went and found a "spark" who also helped reinforce my belief that I don't deserve the love that feels boring.

Thank you for writing this, I can't wait to follow you
on your own journey!"

- Reader Lucas K., California

"Thank you, Rikki, for all the time and effort
that went into writing this book.
I feel like it's a masterpiece and so very
relevant to me."

- Reader P., United States

–

*For everyone who wants nothing more
than to find the love they dream of
and hold it in their hand.*

–

The Anxious Hearts Guide

Copyright @2021 by Rikki Cloos

AnxiousHeartsGuide.com

Cover illustration by Anchorage, Alaska artist John Jeffrey Schlegel.

6th Edition.

Octopi Publishing Partners
Anchorage, Alaska 99517
OctopiPub.com

Library of Congress Control Number: 2021921042

Anxious Hearts Guide / Rikki Cloos
ISBN: 979-8-9851230-0-5 (Paperback)
ISBN: 979-8-9851230-1-2 (Ebook)

Printed in the United States of America

THE

ANXIOUS HEARTS

GUIDE

RISING ABOVE ANXIOUS ATTACHMENT

RIKKI CLOOS

Acknowledgments

Thank you from the bottom of my anxious heart to everyone
who helped this dream come to fruition.

First and foremost, to my dear friend Nic Skovgaard at AlterEgo Marketing, without whom
this book would never have come to be; I wouldn't have even had the guts to start.
On January 1, 2021, you challenged me to write a book. Naturally, I resisted, saying
that it was impossible. I will never forget your sarcastic response:
"You're right. You couldn't possibly write a book! You'd need to have a writing degree,
a design degree, marketing experience, and a well-researched topic that you're insanely
passionate about…oh well!" My friend, this book would not exist if you had not convinced me
that I could write it. From the day that we met back in 2012, you have always been an
amazing confidant, coach, and friend to me…I could not possibly thank you enough.

To my partner, Chris—thank you for loving me through my anxious attachment journey.
You've taught me so, so much. We've learned so much together and your
support and strength have helped me grow into someone I'm proud to be.
You push me through my fear when I'm afraid by giving me confidence that
I don't yet have. I hope that the skills I've learned on this journey can help me properly
thank you for all that you've given me. Your endless encouragement, creative ideas,
and steadfast support are just a few of the many, many things that I love, respect,
and admire about you.

To my mom and my sister—you are my biggest cheerleaders. Your advice,
unwavering enthusiasm, and encouragement pushed me through procrastination,
writer's block, and imposter syndrome. I love and appreciate you both so much.

To my son Carter—thank you for your excitement, creativity, love, and support.
You were so patient and supportive while I spent long afternoons and evenings typing away
on this. I hope you know how incredibly proud of you I am (and always will be. ;-)

To my friends and everyone who patiently sat through my endless stories about attachment
theory, writing, Instagram, and all things relationship-related; thank you for being there for me
in my darkest days of anxiety and attachment woes. Thank you for the insights into your own
relationships and anxieties. I absolutely treasure the time that I get to connect with each of you
and cannot imagine my life without each of your unique, wonderful brains to converse with!

And to all of the Anxious Hearts Guide community on Instagram:
thank you for joining me in the journey toward secure attachment.
Your words, thoughts, and messages have the power to make all anxious attachers
feel less alone, supported, and hopeful about a romantic future that can be
more like we dream it could be.

IDENTIFYING THE PROBLEM

BUILDING SELF-WORTH

CREATING YOUR BEST LIFE

BECOMING SECURE

ESTABLISHING HEALTHY LOVE

Conclusion

Resources

"YOU CANNOT CHANGE YOUR FUTURE, BUT YOU CAN CHANGE YOUR HABITS, AND SURELY YOUR HABITS WILL CHANGE YOUR FUTURE."

DR. ABDUL KALAM

INTRODUCTION

So you're single. Again.

Maybe you're newly single, fresh off the heels of a(nother!?) failed relationship? Maybe you're chronically single, never able to turn a connection
into something that lasts? Or maybe the whole dating pool is just a mirage
that seems to vanish whenever you get close enough to let yourself have
hope.

Where have all the good ones gone?

Maybe you're not single but you're miserable in your relationship,
situationship, "friends with benefits," or whatever you call the unsatisfying
romantic setup you're currently in. Maybe you've been with your partner for
a long time and have never felt that you were able to get them as close as
you need them to be? (Maybe this isn't describing you at all, but I'll bet you
know or love someone who is like this. You may have seen them struggling
and weren't sure what kind of advice to give them.)

I'm here to lay an uncomfortable truth on you, reader, so brace yourself.

There is a distinct possibility that your own behavior is pushing away the very thing you seek.

How could that be!? I want a big, exciting love. Doesn't everyone?
Aren't I just making bad choices in finding people who aren't right for me?
Maybe if I could just find the right person, everything would fall into place and I could be happy.

Well...

A long time ago, I read a quote that really resonated with me. It was something awful that I couldn't unsee. It was a cold, hard truth that made me feel like I was waking up from a long nightmare of disillusionment, finger pointing, and my own personal pity party of victimhood.

The single common denominator in all of your failed relationships...is you.

I'm not trying to hurt your feelings. And if you think about it, this is actually great news. If the problem was everyone else, you'd be faced with the challenge of finding the rare diamond in the rough. It would be a problem of numbers and the answer would be to simply continue putting yourself through nerve-wracking date after date until you get lucky and find *The One*. But consider this; if *you're* the underlying problem, it's not just bad luck preventing you from finding a great match. It means that you've been missing diamonds all around you because as it turns out, you yourself are a little rough.

Have you been told that you're too clingy? Or maybe too picky? Do you walk on eggshells, afraid that you will be abandoned if you make the wrong move? Do warning bells go off in your head when you feel that your partner or love interest is pulling away? Perhaps you have trouble talking about your needs *(what if my needs scare them away!?)* so you hide them or express them indirectly. Most of all, you just want love and it feels like no one ever gets as close as you'd like. Or alternatively, they get *too* close too soon.

Check, check, and check. If *any* of these ring a bell (or you hear a whole lot of ringing bells right now), I hate to say it, but your biggest problem in dating is likely…you.

You may have even suspected this. But hey! Don't shoot the messenger! Read on, friend. I have good news.

With some polishing in the form of hard work, a perspective change, and a little bit of elbow grease, you can reveal your inner diamond as well. And *that's* something that everyone who has been passing you up, overlooking you, or treating you like a sad, unappealing lump of coal will be able to see and appreciate too.

So who am I to tell you these things?

Well, reader, I'm you. From the future.

I have been where you are and I know how much it sucks. The frustration. The shame. The anxiety and feelings of hopelessness. *Will I EVER get this relationship stuff right!?*

On that note, years ago, I found myself suddenly and unexpectedly divorced.

Our decision to divorce was so sudden that I think it took both of us by surprise, too. The intense emotional turmoil that followed my divorce (which was amicable, but still incredibly painful) was sudden, overwhelming, and unexpected (I cannot even begin to imagine the hell that an acrimonious divorce must be). I'd lay awake at night wondering why and how I had found myself alone after twelve partnered years. I agonized over what was wrong with me. The aftermath of my divorce was not difficult due to any fighting, drama, or verbal attacks, but rather, having to finally face *myself* and my own relationship struggles for the very first time.

To my shock, this experience turned out to be a giant blessing in disguise.

I've found that after a breakup, we can easily lose ourselves in distractions; food or drink or nights out with friends. We can hop right back into the dating pool, wading through new faces and excitement and disappointments big enough to distract from any pesky emotions that a breakup may inspire. And while people find plenty of effective distractions post-divorce as well, the crushing feeling of failure after the termination of a marriage is much harder to ignore. It's big enough, expensive enough, and emotionally messy enough that it's hard not to sit yourself down and ask, *"How can I prevent this from ever happening to me again?"*

And this, friends, is where I found big change.

But first, I had a few major missteps to make.

Foolishly, like many new divorcees, I started dating as soon as I could— which is to say, *much* too soon after my divorce.

Dating was a beast I was not prepared to face. I met lots of guys who thought I was cute and seemed to enjoy my company. I had no problem finding fun, entertaining dates. Truth be told, I seemed to be doing better than most in the dating pool. So why was I having such a miserable time? There wasn't a problem if I didn't see any relationship potential in my date. But as soon as I felt myself feeling interested in a guy, the internal torture began. I'd worry, obsess, water down my words, needs, boundaries, and expectations. I would hope against hope that they liked me, that they were the one who would finally choose me, only to find that everyone who I was seriously interested in would vanish or just hang around casually and refuse to commit. Why did I lose myself so completely the second I caught the dreaded "feels?" And why were the ones I actually liked so terrified of settling down with me?

What was wrong with me? And why did I feel so...*unlovable?* Is this your question, too?

When I started this journey, I thought that my relationship anxieties and needs were 100% real and justified. I couldn't imagine why everyone thought the things that I wanted were unreasonable or "too much." But the more I dove into my research on attachment theory, couples counseling, and the psychology around relationship anxiety, the more I realized that my anxieties and needs weren't necessarily so cut and dried.

And even more frightening: I discovered that they were not necessarily so reasonable either.

17

Don't get me wrong! My thoughts and needs were real in the way that thoughts are real, physical things caused by electrical wirings and firings in the brain that increase our heart rate and make us sweat and shake. But when I took a closer look I found that my fears were mostly unfounded. They were also grossly exaggerated. I, like you (or someone you love who struggles in this way), possessed a brain wired to be on high-alert for any sign of disconnection or abandonment, real or imagined.

You don't have to be freshly divorced for this to be your story. I have friends of all ages, of different genders, and with varying levels of dating experience, who complain of this same problem. The dating forums online are filled to the brim with questions posted by high school and college students, twenty-, thirty-, forty-, and fifty-somethings, divorcees, retirees; people from all walks of life in the dating pool.

Why don't I like the ones who like me?
Why don't the ones I like ever like me back?
Why do I fall apart as soon as I start feeling things?

Anxious Heart, (that's my term for us anxious folks who can't seem to find the love we want so badly) bear with me. This story *can* turn around!

If you don't identify as an Anxious Heart, the chances are good that someone you love does. We make up somewhere between 20–25% of the general population. This book aims to help struggling Anxious Hearts, or those who love and support them, understand how their attachment style is affecting their dating/relationship experience and discover healthy ways to handle/heal anxious attachment.

I've probably always been an Anxious Heart, myself. But even before I discovered attachment theory and identified my own style, I knew that the way I'd been doing things wasn't working. When I discovered the concept of attachment theory, I resolved to face my dating problems head-on and attack the issue of insecure attachment until I understood it inside and out.

Call me an overachiever, if you will, but that's how I do things.

Instead of continuing to beat my head against the wall, I found a therapist who understood and challenged me. I committed wholeheartedly to the hard work of turning away from the blame game and facing my contribution to my divorce and failed dating situations. I bought a journal and wrote daily for years. I read over 60 books on relationship psychology, self-esteem, self-compassion, and interpersonal conflict and communication, all in the first two years after my divorce! I devoured the content produced by leaders in the field of relationship dynamics and self-betterment. On a daily basis I pushed myself physically and mentally until slowly, little by little, I noticed that I began to think and feel differently about myself and the relationships I was in.

Before long, there was no more denying it; my efforts were working. Little by little, my life began to feel easier and happier. Relationship stress began to dissipate. My friendships felt more effortless and authentic. I started to communicate about things that mattered to me that I used to stuff down and hide. I would look back on journal entries from my darker days and not recognize the person writing the entries.

I found myself in a relationship that was strangely getting *better* all the time...!

And all those things meant that I *wasn't* stuck and that real change was not only possible but within my grasp!

We aren't doomed by our attachment style. And even better, knowing it can help us find the keys to unlock the cage that keeps us stuck in unsatisfying relationships and situations.

I wanted to tell everyone I knew! I wanted to tell everyone I didn't know! I began brainstorming on how I could help everyone who was struggling with anxiety, low self-esteem, and self-abandonment in relationships. The escape hatch from all of the worry, intrusive thoughts, self-defeating behavior, and poor treatment from relationship partners was open for me and I wanted to help other people open that same door too.

I want to help you open that door.

Everything you dream of within a relationship (love, affection, security, mutuality, reciprocity, etc.) is within your reach and the only thing holding you back is *you*.

Am I a perfect, self-actualized person who has solved all of their relationship woes and never experiences discomfort, dissatisfaction, or trouble because I have everything figured out?

Of course not! *(Spoiler alert: those people don't exist. Even the happiest and most secure couples experience anxiety and relationship trouble from time to time.)*

But I do believe that through research, reading, and hard work I've figured out quite a few tools and mindsets that have massively improved my life, increased my own happiness, and positively affected everyone I interact with. Oh, it's also made dating and relationships a lot more manageable and dare I say *fun*.

It's my conviction that the sobering moment when you can take a good hard look at *yourself* is the beginning of a beautiful new relationship (with yourself) and that this is the solution to your daily relationship anxiety.

And the most amazing thing (that no one believes when I tell them) is that at the end of your journey, your fear of dying alone could be much reduced thanks to having designed a full, meaningful, satisfying life for yourself in the process—whether partnered or not. You'll also get so much more satisfaction from your relationships (romantic or platonic) that you may finally be able to focus on other aspects of your life. You won't feel compelled to work on solving your relationship problems 24/7, 365 days of the year.

Ideally, you'll be busy making your own life fantastic, fun, compelling, and *definitely not* something that you want to escape or be saved from.

Can you even imagine!?

Fortunately, it just so happens that this kind of life is exactly the kind of thing that all the diamonds out there in the dating pool are irresistibly attracted to.

Do you worry that you're either 'not enough' or 'too much?' Do you hope that someone will 'pick you' before you even get a chance to know them? Do you come running when a prospective romantic partner calls?

Or do you have enough going on that they need to put in some real effort in order to get your attention?

Your answer to questions like that may very well determine whether or not someone sticks around.

In the chapters ahead, we're going to identify the problem (your attachment style), repair your self-esteem (the foundation of having a good relationship), build your best life (making it full, attractive, and fun), do the hard work (breaking the pattern of dysfunction and/or insecure attachment), and finally—only when you're ready—prepare you to jump back into the dating pool as a much better swimmer.

All of the work you'll find within these pages aims to culminate in your glorious re-entry into the dating pool (and life!) feeling more secure and grounded, more confident about what you want, and more ready to face your attachment fears.

No need to skip to the end of the book. Here's the secret right up front: it's not actually *you* that is the problem; I'm sure that you're amazing and lovable. The problem is in your *thoughts about yourself* and *your behavior*. Somewhere, deep down, you may know this. But even knowing this, how do you go about fixing it?

Buckle up, my friend. I'm really, truly glad you're here. It's not going to be easy. It's probably not going to be fun, either. In fact, most of this journey is downright challenging. But the good news is that I do have some answers for you.

There will be tears, setbacks, and big, uncomfortable emotions.

Brace yourself for two-steps-forward, three-steps-back, and growth that will be exciting but painful at times.

I know—I'm really selling it, huh?

But if you're doing it right, there will also be big mental changes that will make you question how you've been living this entire time. Light bulb moments. The feeling that you're slowly 'leveling up.' Prepare for friends and family to notice a new glow about you, a confidence they haven't seen in awhile, if ever before. Consider the thrilling moment when your partner or new date openly compliments your independence and *joie de vivre*! (Bonus points if they use that phrase!)

Additionally, be prepared for the moments where you try to tell yourself that you're finished with the hard work even though you still have a ways to go. (You won't be finished, but don't worry, we'll talk about how to identify that, too!)

If you're feeling skeptical right now, hang in there. But please trust me when I tell you that it's all undeniably, unequivocally, 100% *worth it*. You're going to thank yourself when you get to the other side.

Sincerely, your future self, and a former anxious heart

THE ROOT OF SUFFERING IS ATTACHMENT.

THE BUDDHA

CHAPTER ONE

IDENTIFYING THE PROBLEM

If you're here, reading this book, chances are good that you're an anxious attacher, and even if you aren't familiar with that quote, you may know *exactly* why I chose it to kick things off.

For us Anxious Hearts, romantic attachment can be rough.

Wouldn't life be so much easier if we could just forget about all of this romance business?

For people like us, relationship anxiety is at the root of our suffering. We can be preoccupied by our thoughts about how to get the people we love closer to us, stop them from pulling away, and feel reassured that they aren't going anywhere. It can make it difficult to sleep, eat, or work. Our attachment anxieties can make our typical routine feel almost impossible.

If this sounds all-too-familiar, you might be an anxious attacher.

If you're not one, the chances are good that you probably care about one—after all, we are roughly 20%–25% of the population. So whether you're familiar with the term "anxious attachment" or not, let's dive into a little background on attachment theory. Knowledge is power, after all, and knowing *why* we do the things that we do helps to demystify the way our brains handle relationship attachment so that we can take control of our troublesome behavior.

This kind of knowledge could also make your conversation more interesting at cocktail parties or on dates. At the very least, it can't hurt!

The Strange Situation Test

Back in the 1960s, a British psychoanalyst named John Bowlby (1907–1990) developed the Theory of Attachment to help explain how people connect to others emotionally. He described two ways of relating to the people we're closest to: securely and insecurely. Secure folks are comfortable with intimacy, good at calming themselves down, and are better with vulnerability too.

Confident, open, and relationally healthy, roughly half of the population are secure attachers. Lucky dogs!

The other half of the population, the insecure attachers, are divided almost equally between the "anxious preoccupied" and the "dismissive avoidant" attachers. When I describe these two groups to people who have not heard of attachment theory, I'll sometimes refer to the two attachment styles as the "clingers" and the "runners," respectively. This is how you would recognize these types in books or movies. But this crude way of describing insecure attachment is far too simplified and doesn't do this complex behavior any justice.

To give you an appreciation for the complexity, I'll go into more detail about each attachment type. But first, some background on the experiment in which the attachment styles were discovered.

Mary Ainsworth, a colleague of John Bowlby, ran a famous experiment in 1967 called the Strange Situation Test that provides a fantastic illustration of the three main types (secure, anxious preoccupied, and avoidant.)[1]

In the experiment, a baby between the ages of 12-months and 18-months enters an observation room with its mother. In the room are toys, a one-way mirror (for researchers to make their observations) and a seated stranger. After a moment in the room, the mother is instructed to exit and leave the baby in the room with the stranger while the researcher notes the child's behavior during that time. Finally, the mother is instructed to return to her baby in the room.

The researchers noted three distinct ways that the babies in the study responded to the separation and reunion.

Secure attachment was proved when the child would explore the toys upon entering the room, but would become distressed upon finding their mother gone. They might then cry or search for her. Upon her return, the child is reassured of its safety and easily calmed. This behavior from around 50% of the children in the study showed that the child had a high level of

---

1 Ainsworth, M. (1978). "The Bowlby-Ainsworth attachment theory." Behavioral and Brain Sciences, 1(3), 436–438. doi: 10.1017/s0140525x00075828.

trust in their mother, and depended on her for their safety. As a very young, defenseless child, the disappearance of our parental attachment figure *should* bother us. Imagine how much danger a lone or orphaned child in prehistoric times would be in. In the same vein, a parent's reappearance should be very reassuring. These securely attached children grow up to be adults who trust the ones that they love. They feel sure that when their loved ones "disappear" they will come back providing safety, love, and support.

Secure attachers are able to relate romantically in healthy, independent, *and* interdependent ways. They make phenomenal partners, parents, and friends because they are comfortable with intimacy and secure in how they relate to those who are close to them.

But this was only one-half of the children in the study. What about the other half? Let's take a look at you, Anxious Hearts.

'Insecure' attachment in the form of the **anxious preoccupied** showed up in around 20% of the children in the study. This style was identified by the child who would not explore the toys in the room and would cling to their mother instead. When left alone with the stranger, this child became extremely distressed and difficult or impossible to calm down upon their mother's return. This child did not trust that their mother would return, or that she would stay even after she came back. The child had an anxious, nervous demeanor and seemed constantly on the lookout (preoccupied) for signs of abandonment or emotional detachment.

The children with this attachment style were hyper-aware of what their loved ones were doing, feeling, and thinking because being able to predict their behavior meant staying ahead of any abandonment. They would grow into adults who were clingy, boundary-pushing, codependent, and nervous in intimate relationships. (Does this sound familiar?)

Insecure attachment in the form of the **avoidant attacher** presented itself in about 25% of children studied. These children appeared completely unfazed by their mother's leaving, and looked equally uninterested in her return to the room. Further, they showed little interest in the toys in the room as well. Sadly, looks can be deceiving. This lackluster response didn't mean that the child was strong and independent. Rather, a strong stress response was raging inside, similar in intensity to the anxiously attached children... but the child either doesn't notice it, or doesn't show it.

Avoidantly attached children learned that their cries of distress and protest weren't rewarded with comfort. Worse, some were punished or shamed for showing sadness/fear/excessive needs. They quickly learned to stop trying to elicit attention. These children also did not feel empowered to independently explore the toys in the room upon entrance; instead, they would sit quietly, reserved, and/or feigning disinterest.

Avoidantly attached adults are detached in relationships, unconsciously ignoring their own and others' emotional needs. Another term for this type was **dismissive avoidant**, in reference to how they dismiss their own and others' emotional responses.

The remaining 5% of children displayed a "disorganized" attachment style. Dubbed **fearful avoidants**, they showed the most troublesome characteristics of both the avoidant and anxious children. Like the other insecurely attached children, they did not bravely explore the toys upon entering the room. The most interesting part of the fearful avoidant's behavior was that although they may have cried when their mother disappeared, they did *not* run to her for comfort when she returned. Heartbreakingly, these children would freeze or back away from her upon her return. While feeling unsafe outside of her presence, they also did not trust her as a source of comfort in their distress.

As adults, these individuals do not find comfort in their partners (as the anxiously attached do) *or* in themselves (as avoidants do) and typically become this way as a result of great trauma.

The way that our attachment styles follow us into adulthood define how we relate to our romantic partners. To be sure, our romantic partners are not our mothers. However, our love interests have a way of becoming our primary sources of strength, security, and emotional validation as adults. Because of this, we tend to replace our parental figures with *them* as we make our way out into the world on our own.

And while we don't need our attachment figures with us constantly to protect us from strangers in observation rooms, we do need them to lean on in times of emotional difficulty. And if we learned to relate to them in a dysfunctional way as children, that habit puts an undeniable strain on our romantic relationships as adults. The anxious children will grow up to feel powerless and afraid, as if they can't do anything without their support figure around. The avoidant children retreat into themselves, refusing to ask anyone for help and feeling unsettled when help and love is offered to them. The fearful avoidants, an unfortunate mix of both styles, come to find stress and anxiety whether alone or in the company of their partner.

You can see why this is so serious now, right?

Attachment style isn't specific to gender or sexual preference. It transcends our exterior packaging and finds its roots deep in the brain. The way that we connect with the important people in our lives who calm and soothe us (parents, first, and then romantic partners later in life) transcends sex and sexual preference. I am writing from a cis, heteronormative perspective, but throughout the book, I try to keep things as neutral as possible to relate to a wider audience.

Anxious Hearts come in all shapes, sizes, and flavors. And although the data shows that the majority of anxious attachers are women, there are plenty of men who struggle with it too. The common thread between all of us is the pain and struggle of living with an insecure attachment system and how it touches almost all aspects of our relationships.

Where Our Attachment Style Comes From

There are tons of free tests online if you want to find out which attachment style you have. I'll bet that reading the descriptions above might give you an idea of which attachment style you identify most closely with.

Read the lists below describing the four attachment styles. Do the behaviors or thoughts listed sound familiar? It can be tempting to ask a partner to take a test, or to read these aloud to try to gauge their attachment style. It can also be tempting to blame a partner for the problems in the relationship based on these lists. I ask you to hold off until you've made it through the book. Hopefully, you'll feel very differently about these once we learn more. Until then...which attachment style do you identify with the most?

Anxious Attachment

Constant need for closeness/intimacy.

Hypersensitivity to partner's moods and actions.

Tendency to be controlling when they feel threatened.

Preoccupied by fear of abandonment.

Prioritizes a partner's wants/needs before their own.

Unable to give a partner healthy space.

Over-giving to partner, quick to dismiss their own needs.

Excessive worrying/catastrophizing.

Controlling behavior; requires a partner to prove their loyalty.

Often adopts partner's hobbies/interests to increase closeness.

Feels deeply uncomfortable/unsafe expressing issues.

Becomes overly dependent on their relationship.

Vigilant for signs of abandonment/disloyalty.

Constant need to please/gain approval.

Unaware of/unable to express wants/needs.

Poor sense of boundaries within a relationship.

Requires frequent reassurance of partner's commitment/care.

Lets partner make the rules and set the tone of the relationship.

Believes they must work to keep their partner interested.

Highly jealous; suspects that their partner will be unfaithful.

Has an unrealistic view of how a relationship should be.

Feels uncomfortable receiving intimacy.

Discomfort being single. Often jumps from partner to partner.

Avoidant Attachment

Constant need for autonomy and independence.

Insensitivity to partner's moods and actions.

Tendency to pull away when they sense a partner getting close.

Believes a partner wants more than they can give them.

Pride themselves on not needing anyone.

Tendency to withdraw when they feel threatened.

Preoccupied by fear of enmeshment/being smothered.

Prioritizes own wants/needs before their partner's.

Uncomfortable opening up about private thoughts/feelings.

Minimizes the importance of emotional expression.

Difficulty trusting/relying on others/asking for help.

Believes they don't need emotional intimacy in their life.

Often ignores/diminishes a partner's attempts to increase closeness.

Feels relationships are more work/trouble than they're worth.

Overly rigid with relationship rules/has great difficulty compromising.

Feels that people are always going to let them down.

Overvalues privacy. Acts guarded within a relationship.

Makes derogatory statements about attachment/monogamy.

Feels more comfortable keeping their options open.

Shuts down/explodes when faced directly with conflict.

Appears confident, strong, and in control.

Has an unrealistic view of how a relationship should be.

Uses emotional or physical distancing strategies to keep others at bay.

More comfortable when single. Often hesitant to commit.

Secure Attachment

Healthy need for closeness and independence within a relationship.

Aware of/expresses their wants and needs.

Feels comfortable being their authentic self within a relationship.

Will not stay in a relationship that makes them unhappy.

Comfortable with closeness/independence within their relationship.

Knows they will ultimately be OK if they are rejected.

Healthy sense of boundaries (their own and their partner's).

Can prioritize a partner's wants/needs as well as their own.

Comfortable addressing issues with a partner.

Doesn't require excessive proof of loyalty.

Openly expresses affection for partner.

Has a more realistic view of how a relationship should be.

Can be happy when single or within a relationship.

Does not act out or try to make their partner jealous.

Communicates relationship issues in a healthy way.

Has no trouble compromising.

Is not afraid of commitment.

Feels motivated to get closer when a partner reciprocates.

Introduces friends and family easily.

Comfortable expressing strong feelings within a relationship.

Comfortable giving and receiving intimacy.

Do you identify strongly with any of the attachment types? Maybe one sounds like your partner, or an ex? Now is a good time to grab a bookmark, hop online, and identify your attachment style. There are many fast, free tests online. There is a very short, quick test available at AttachmentProject.com.[2]

2 The Attachment Project: Learn Attachment Theory from Experts

If you would like more comprehensive questioning and to have your test results saved online for re-testing later, create an account over at YourPersonality.net.[3] Don't worry, I'll wait. Or for those defiant types, just keep reading.

If you're reading this book, chances are good that you're probably an anxious attacher or at least lean that way; we as a type tend to be highly motivated and focused on making ourselves "worthy of love" and desire to "abandon-proof" our relationships. Fearful avoidants also have a tendency to be highly motivated for self-improvement; they appear on the attachment theory self-help forums at rates far higher than their established 5%.

The rest of this book will be directed at the mindset and behavior of anxious attachers. They are the crowd for whom this was written, after all. Fearful avoidant attachers will also recognize and resonate with a lot of the content throughout the book. But if you happen to be secure or avoidant, there's plenty for you here, as well. You probably know and love many anxious folks and this guide will be great for understanding them, as well as learning how to love them in ways that don't provoke their anxiety. The content ahead will aid you, too, in your quest for general self-improvement. After all, *everyone* carries some degree of insecurity in love—even the most secure folks. At the very least, this book may help you to understand the buzzing, fascinating mind of the anxiously attached people in your life, even if you happen to be rocking a different attachment style.

So don't toss, shelf or re-gift this book just yet if you aren't among my anxious brethren.

We all carry some anxiety in the search for love and attachment to

---

http://www.attachmentproject.com/
3 YourPersonality.net http://www.yourpersonality.net

another person. The vulnerability required of healthy relationships can be terrifying for healthy, happy people, too! The crushing loneliness of being single is often felt by even the most confident among us.

Our attachment style affects almost everything about how we relate in relationships; how we communicate our emotions and needs to partners, friends, and family; how we respond to conflict; how we view other people's roles in our lives, our expectations/attitudes about others…

We can literally train our brains out of these troublesome patterns; effectively changing our established attachment style.

No matter what your attachment style is, knowing a thing or two about attachment helps us understand and explain patterns in our relationships that might otherwise cause stress or derail connections.

So where does our attachment style come from?

Nice to Meet You! I Am Anxiously Attached

Ideally, our parents are attuned to our needs when we are babies. They feed us when we're hungry, comfort us when we're afraid or in pain, and help introduce us to the world through safe, consistent caretaking. Because of this kind of nurturing, we go on to develop a deep-seated trust in our parents—a feeling of being truly safe from harm and abandonment.

Oh, to be naturally secure. Alas, not all of us are so lucky.

Inconsistent care (alternately nurturing and then cold, critical, or emotionally unavailable parents) can wreak havoc on a baby's perception of the world as being the kind of place that meets their needs. This creates a nervous or detached child. They may always be on guard for ways to get their needs met. They may be easily upset, whiny, and attention-seeking. What other way could a child get its needs met when they may be ignored or abandoned if they let themselves go unnoticed?

On the avoidant side, what incentive does a child have to cry out if that cry is met with punishment, shaming, or dismissal?

Wait a minute! I hear you saying. *Knock it off! My parents weren't so bad!*

I promise that I'm not trying to trash-talk your parents. It doesn't do any good to condemn all the parents of insecurely attached children. Consider the parent suffering from a crippling depression who is unable to notice or tend to her child's loneliness. Imagine a military father stationed overseas who can't physically be there to give his son a hug when he feels afraid. Or consider the plight of the overlooked middle child in a family of five who feels forgotten and unnoticed by overworked, overwhelmed parents.

Life, more often than not, is far from the easy utopia that we wish all children could grow up in. And further, I believe that most parents are doing the best they can with the tools at their disposal.

Additionally, genetics may also play a part. Anxiety disorders can cause the babies and children of even very attentive parents to be naturally on edge—feeling afraid or wound up by even the slightest neglect that they perceive. Their extra-sensitive nervous systems are always on high alert for a parent not noticing hair-trigger needs. They can then carry that fear and hyper-vigilance into their adult lives. This can manifest as the imagined fear that their romantic partners are also unable to soothe them and may disappear at any moment. Or think of the naturally less sensitive child who can't hear their own internal alarms. They, too, might grow up imagining that the world doesn't care about their needs.

After all, if parenting were 100% to blame, siblings would share the exact same attachment style and they most certainly don't.

Our attachment styles can also come from traumatic bonding experiences we have as teens or adults (abandonment, abuse, bereavement, divorce, infidelity, etc.) These events can shape how you show up in intimate relationships, as well! But thankfully, this means that our attachment styles are not as concrete as we may fear. Therapy, hard work, and external influences can help move insecure attachers closer to being securely attached. This wonderful fact is one of the primary reasons I decided to write this very book!

In 'Getting the Love You Want', Dr. Harville Hendrix and his coauthor/wife Helen describe the concept of neuroplasticity. They write that we have "social brains" that are continuously influenced by all of our relationships. In one of my favorite sentences from the book, they write: "Your brain is changed every time you interact with others." As an author, educator, public lecturer, and therapist with more than thirty years experience, Dr Harville and his wife go on to explain how every experience we have is recorded in our brains as a chemical pathway linking individual nerve cells.

Unfortunately, very painful experiences are recorded as extra strong pathways. And each time you have a similar painful experience these pathways are etched even deeper into your brain.[4] But thanks to neuroplasticity, we're far from doomed. We can literally train our brains out of these troublesome patterns effectively changing our established attachment style.

So as you can see, attachment can be pretty complicated. But not hopeless! And on that note, let's focus less on *how* it happened and more on *what we can do about it*, shall we?

So Which Type Am I?

If you aren't an anxious attacher, the following may be difficult to wrap your head around. On the other hand, if you lean toward this attachment style, prepare to feel very seen and understood, if not just a tad bit called out.

For the anxiously attached, relationships are *hard*. Anxious Hearts, I know you feel me when I say this. It's almost maddening how we tend to climb right back on the roller coaster that throws us around so violently.

From the moment we decide that someone could be special to us, our brain kicks into overdrive. At first, it can feel absolutely amazing. Being an anxious attacher in the early stages of infatuation and attachment feels like getting drunk, going crazy, and riding a sugar-high simultaneously. There's intrigue, excitement, fantasies of how things could be, wild scheming and the like.

Before we even know what hit us, plans start materializing, text messages are flying, future children are numbered and named. And this can happen as early as "the talking stage," before we even meet the object of our desire!

---

4 Hendrix, Harville, and Helen Hunt. Getting the Love You Want: A Guide for Couples. Simon & Schuster UK Ltd., 2020.

We are the ultimate dreamers. Think Romeo. Think children plucking petals from flowers. We're the helpless, hopeless romantics who while away our hours listening to sappy music or writing poetry on our beds and hoping that our beloved feels the same way about us. That is, until the *slightest* sign that they don't. And it's at that moment that things suddenly don't seem so sunny.

Hearing what I call the "warning bells" of attachment anxiety is, quite simply, hell.

It can happen when they take too long to text us back. It's the slight hesitation in their voice when they accept your invitation for a date. It's a "like" on someone else's photo, a text notification from deep in their pocket that they don't check in front of you, their failure to look up when you point something out to them, or when they simply forget to ask you how your day went. It's the sinking feeling you get when they're gone too long, when they don't invite you over, when they don't want to talk about something that's bothering them, when they leave without saying goodbye...

(How's your blood pressure, anxious attachers? Are you still with me!?)

Any one of these things can set off those warning bells. And if you're familiar with them then you know that they are *loud*.

The warning bells defy logic. Even if we know that what we're feeling upset about isn't realistic, the bells are too loud to ignore. Our heart rate jumps and we may start to sweat or shake. The intrusive thoughts pile up, repeat, and overshadow all other thoughts. Little lines crease our forehead and the words "is anything wrong?" are already out before we can stop them.

And it begins; the plight of the anxious attacher is in full bloom. It's our never-ending self-fulfilling prophecy that we perpetuate ad nauseum.

"Can we talk?"

"I haven't heard from you in a few hours. Are you mad at me?"

"When can I see you again?"

"Did I do something wrong?"

"Why did they pull away?"

We worry that our relationships will end, and our relationships end because we worry too much.

I see you, Anxious Heart. And I am delighted to tell you that *love doesn't have to be this way for you.*

The Signs of Anxious Attachment

Anxious folks have a hard (read: impossible) time feeling secure in a relationship. They cling to the object of their affection, looking for constant reassurance that they will not be abandoned. In addition to that, there is an excessive need for validation and affection as a means of comfort/reassurance. Because they are unable to self-regulate and calm the warning bells when it feels like their partner is pulling away, they feel they are at the mercy of their partner, waiting to be reassured and saved from their own anxiety.

Here are some of the hallmark behaviors of this attachment style:

- Clingy, needy behavior
- Overanalyzing and constantly worrying about your relationship
- Putting the needs of others before your own, always

- Constant, insatiable craving for closeness and intimacy
- Intolerance for your partner being unavailable or inattentive
- The tendency to lose yourself in relationships
- Codependency
- Difficulty being alone
- Low self-esteem/No sense of self
- Frequently indulging in oversharing/gossip
- Strong fear of rejection/criticism/abandonment
- Needing constant reassurance that you are cared about
- Being overly affected by your partner's actions/moods
- A tendency toward moodiness, impulsivity, and instability
- Prone to jealousy, insecurity, and unhealthy coping mechanisms

How many of these sound familiar? How many would your partner say that you struggle with? Are you a fellow Anxious Heart?

Any one of these behaviors can strain a normal, healthy relationship. But the sad truth of anxious attachment is that often many of these are present at once. At extreme levels, an anxious attacher can struggle with *every single bullet point.* This kind of behavior has the potential to derail any relationship it's found in. Not even the healthiest, most stable partner is immune to the destabilizing power of a truly Anxious Heart. This is why it's so important to address the problem of an insecure attachment style. When these kinds of relational behaviors start to become a regular part of how you interact with people, all of your relationships (even platonic ones!) are strained.

People who struggle greatly with insecure attachment can find themselves less happy in their relationships in general, be they romantic, platonic, familial, or in the workplace. They report relationships as feeling more stressful, painfully emotional, and less stable.

So how come the insecurely attached cannot seem to conduct themselves in relationships the same way that secure attachers can? The difference is in the problematic way that insecure attachers view their relationships, paired with damaging communication strategies that feel perfectly normal to us insecure types. We have a tendency to stress out the secure folks in our lives who don't use these unhealthy methods of communicating but must deal with ours.

So what does it look like when two insecure attachers pair up?

The Push-Pull Dynamic/the Anxious-Avoidant Trap

Anxious attachers often function perfectly fine in non-romantic relationships. They can be confident, assertive, exercise healthy boundaries, etc. We also tend to be very loving and sensitive; friends and family might describe us as "givers" who are always looking out for others. So why is it that romantic relationships are so much more difficult for us? What makes romantic relationships different?

Enter "the anxious-avoidant trap."

In a cruel twist of fate, anxious attachers most often find themselves in relationships with their most challenging possible counterpart: avoidants.

Clingers and runners.
The pursuer and the pursued.
Cat and mouse.

However you want to describe them, these two are irresistibly drawn to each other time and time again and the dance of dysfunction begins. In her wonderful book on Emotionally Focused Therapy for couples, Dr. Sue Johnson refers to the harmful ways that anxious and avoidants communicate as 'Demon Dialogues.'[5] If you've gone through this before, this should sound uncomfortably familiar.

She refers to one of her Demon Dialogues as The Protest Polka. In this interaction, the anxious partner spends their energy trying to get closer to the avoidant, who in turn pours their energy into resisting all of these attempts. Occasionally, a brief connection will be made; an avoidant will allow a moment or two of tender affection, a sizzling sexual connection will sometimes fan the flames, or a trail of breadcrumbs will be left for the anxious attacher who desperately hopes that someday they will win the avoidant over and finally experience the love that they dream of.

After a moment/day/week of closeness or connection, the avoidant is activated by their own fears, and works hard to put physical or emotional distance between the two in order to feel safe again. This, in turn, activates the fears of the anxious partner who goes into overdrive trying to bridge the gap. And round and round they go.

Surprisingly, *both* of the participants here (anxious and avoidants alike) crave intimacy but are terrified of it, and the appeal of the relationship for them both is the fact that true closeness never comes about.

But wait! I can already hear you saying. *I'm not terrified of intimacy! I want it more than anything! It's these resistant, distant, commitment-phobic people I choose to date who are the problem!*

5 Johnson, Sue. Hold Me Tight: Your Guide to the Most Successful Approach to Building Loving Relationships. Piatkus, 2011.

I also found myself resistant when I discovered that a taste for emotionally unavailable people signals emotional unavailability in ourselves. It was one of the more difficult truths that I had to face on my journey. So sit down, open your mind, and consider a few of the following points.

- Do you tend to reject potential partners who are very loving/eager to date? Do they seem boring or uninteresting to you?
- Do you struggle with intimacy in its more intense forms (e.g. eye contact during sex, handholding, public displays of affection, talking about what you really want, revealing secrets or dark truths about yourself to your beloved, letting your partner or love interest see your faults, etc.)
- Is the thought of a partner who is easily loving, committed, or dedicated either scary or repulsive to you? Or does the thought of finding someone like this seem unrealistic?
- Do you doubt your ability to keep or please someone worthy of your affection?

Now, if you will, consider how your current or previous partners who seemed so distant allowed you to avoid working on these bullet points. A partner who is cold or unavailable won't make you uncomfortable with profuse affection. They aren't beating down your door to spend time with you or telling you how beautiful you are. They aren't giving you things that you *think* you want but may have run from in the past.

Aren't the amorous, enthusiastic people the ones that you tend to stick firmly in the dreaded Friend Zone? Their efforts feel like "too much." Or they seem "boring." Or you feel things are "too easy."

"I don't know," you often find yourself telling your friends after a date. *"I just didn't feel that spark."*

Unfortunately, many times the spark we're referring to comes from "the chase." And FYI: it's not a healthy thing to seek.

Why do we do this? Perhaps because the unavailable partner is a mystery. They're an enigma to be solved or a prize to be won. Their love, attention, or affection must be *earned* and you're always up for the challenge. And therein lies the key to why you cannot tear yourself away. Their disinterest in you *affirms* your belief that you, as you are now, *are not enough*. It also gives you the chance to try to prove your worthiness to them. This may be a pattern that appears over and over again in your relationships.

So while you desperately wish that they would just give in and give you the love you've been craving, their constant disinterest confirms your deeply held belief that you aren't worthy of the love you crave and also protects you from having to face your own unacknowledged intimacy issues.

A potential partner who is willing to love you *as you are* doesn't match up with how you feel about yourself. *Why should they love me? I haven't done anything to deserve their love.* Both the anxious and avoidant attacher believe that love is scarce and must be earned. Without effort and strife, the love and attention directed toward us doesn't feel justified, real, or safe. The anxious attacher believes that love shouldn't be easy. Our culture glorifying love as pain, self-sacrifice, and struggle only solidifies our feelings that if it's too easy, it isn't worth it.

So the person you have to chase, capture, and impress fuels your fire, and the one who accepts you as you are feels dull, unsatisfying, and too easy. What do you do with that?

I don't have to tell you how frustrating this can be. The unhealthy pull toward partners who are forever pulling away is what makes anxious attachment so miserable. Anyone who experiences this is nodding right now, while everyone else is scratching their head. *"Why would you keep chasing someone who doesn't want you?"* Even those who intimately know the pull of the elusive avoidant partner may also question their motive. As it turns out, there's quite a bit of research that has gone into the reasoning behind that pull.

Prepare yourself and put your science pants on.

Why It's So Hard to Quit Chasing Love

For the insecurely attached, dysfunction in love is quite literally addictive. Encounters, thoughts, and images of our beloved trigger the release of neurochemicals. There's dopamine, the reward neurotransmitter that fires when we eat chocolate or take drugs or have sex (read: very addictive!). There's oxytocin, sometimes referred to as the 'cuddle chemical" that pushes us to bond with others when it is released. You'll find this hormone coursing through our bodies in great amounts during orgasm or breastfeeding. It also has powerful anxiety-relieving properties. Then there's the stressful-feeling vasopressin, raising our blood pressure and making us feel selectively aggressive to defend or fight for our beloved. This one is responsible for making us feel crabby or uncomfortable in love sometimes. This hormone is also a big part of why insecure attachment is tough to handle; real physical changes occur in our bodies when faced with the darker side of love!

The potent cocktail of dopamine, oxytocin, and vasopressin that we're given in toxic, turbulent relationships can have a pull similar to a drug addiction.

Looking back toward attachment theory, it's also interesting to note that when the relationship of an insecurely attached person feels threatened (by distance or disconnect or emotional upset), similar regions of the brain fire as when someone is in physical danger. Your brain is saying, "Pay attention! Our very survival is threatened here!" This is precisely why those "warning bells" are so loud and tough to ignore.

Our body and brain thinks that separation from our beloved is a matter of life or death. Why is this?

For a baby or child, separation from our mother was quite literally a matter of life or death. It was in our best interest as infants to quickly develop the tools to keep ourselves bonded to her. Crying, searching for her, feeling reassured of her love and attention, all of these things helped to ensure our very survival. When this feeling is transferred to a romantic attachment figure as an adult, it's no wonder that separation or disconnection can feel like life or death. As far as your body is concerned, the threat level feels the same!

When the anxious attacher feels their connection with their beloved threatened, their nervous system flies into action. The alarms sound. *Pay attention! This is a life or death situation!* For the anxious attacher, this alarm system is the first line of defense against separation or disconnection. The inner workings of this alarm system include what psychologists call "activating strategies."

Activating Strategies

The body doesn't like feeling a dip in the "feel-good" chemicals in regard to our love interests (attachment figures). Activating strategies are thoughts or feelings that motivate us to reconnect, or allow us to feel physically or emotionally close to the object of our affection.

Some examples of these are:

- Thinking about your beloved or having difficulty concentrating on anything else
- Remembering only their positive qualities
- Putting them on a pedestal (devaluing your good qualities and forgetting their bad ones)
- Believing that your beloved is rare and special, perhaps your only shot at real love
- Getting in contact with them, despite your better judgment, to soothe your anxiety

When your connection feels threatened, your brain compels you to reestablish contact for reassurance or affection. When we are activated and feeling this compulsion, it can feel like losing control. We can feel powerless to stop ourselves from sending that desperate text or making that call at 1:30am. When activating strategies get us feeling sufficiently fired up, it is at this point that the anxious attacher resorts to what psychologists call **protest behavior**.

Protest Behaviors

Even the most securely attached will raise some alarms when their connection with their beloved falters.

"Why are you so late getting home?"
"Will you call me when you get off work?"
"I'm lonely tonight. Can I come over?"

Reconnecting when things feel distant is a normal part of a healthy relationship dynamic. Insecure attachers, however, take these behaviors to the extreme.

Levine and Heller in their book *Attached* have a great list of the protest behaviors of the anxiously attached:

- Calling, texting, or e-mailing many times, waiting for a phone call, loitering by your partner's workplace in hopes of running into him/her.
- Withdrawing: Sitting silently "engrossed" in the paper, literally turning your back on your partner, not speaking, talking with other people on the phone and ignoring him/her.
- Keeping score: Paying attention to how long it took them to return your phone call and waiting just as long to return theirs; waiting for them to make the first "make up" move and acting distant until such time.
- Acting hostile: Rolling your eyes when they speak, looking away, getting up and leaving the room while they're talking (acting hostile can transgress to outright violence at times).
- Threatening to leave: "We're not getting along, I don't think I can

do this anymore." "I knew we weren't right for each other," "I'll be better off without you"—all the while hoping they will stop you from leaving/come crawling back saying they'll change.

- Manipulation: Acting busy or unapproachable. Ignoring phone calls, saying you have plans when you don't.
- Making him/her feel jealous: Making plans to get together with an ex for lunch, going out with friends to a singles bar, telling your partner about someone who flirted with you.

In addition to these behaviors, many anxiously attached women and men use sex as an irresistible tactic to bait a partner into reestablishing contact and closeness. Anxious Hearts who use sex as a weapon to gain closeness may appear hyper-sexual, as they are rewarded with *an extra dopamine boost* when they are successful. They get to enjoy the natural feel-good chemicals from the sexual encounter, as well as the high they get from the anxiety relief that contact with their love object provides.

Avoidant readers and/or partners of Anxious Hearts, take heart that this behavior is far from intentional. Your anxious partner is reacting to a brain screaming out for connection, and it just so happens that sex is often the most reliable way to reestablish the connection with an avoidant who isn't so easily swayed by words.

Have you ever been described as "high maintenance"?

When someone is described as being "high maintenance," it usually means that they are very needy and require excessive communication and reassurance. Do you engage in attention-seeking protest behaviors as described above? These behaviors force a partner to reassure you of their affection. Without your meaning to be, this behavior is manipulative and you can unintentionally push your relationship to its breaking point with frequent behavior like this.

Some of you may be holding this book specifically because you recognize the destructive nature of your protest behavior and want to do something about it. You may be tired of the sense of "stable instability" that insecure relationships bring. You might feel dizzied by the rollercoaster of closeness/intimacy followed by your lover's disappearing act or your own acts of self-sabotage.

The blame in these situations is almost never one-sided. Unfortunately, a partner's unhealthy behavior goes a long way toward provoking an insecure attacher. Your relationship with someone who is secure and communicative is going to feel a lot less volatile and uncertain than a relationship with someone who is also struggling with issues around healthy communication and intimacy.

Anxious Hearts, you feel deeply. That's a beautiful thing; don't try to stop feeling or showing your emotions. Somewhere out there someone exists who appreciates a very deep capacity for love and affection. But until you develop healthy relationship habits (or learn to build them with your current partner) *and* learn to manage the tough parts of your attachment style, a healthy relationship is going to be tough. So what can you do to make things better? This question is even *more* urgent if you're currently in a relationship with a partner who seems resistant to your requests. Take heart:

Insecure attachers (anxious *and* avoidant!) are absolutely capable of becoming secure with education/awareness, hard work, and practice.

Even if your partner is resistant, the work that you do on yourself can change the *entire* atmosphere of your relationship. This encourages growth for your partner by making them feel safe and secure. So, what can you do for yourself? It turns out...a lot! And let me be the first to tell you that the work isn't easy, but it definitely changes the game. Little by little, with consistent effort and gentle self-forgiveness when we backslide, an anxious attacher can move closer to the coveted title of "secure attacher."

Ideally, you are in a relationship with a secure attacher while working on your attachment healing. But, mercifully, you can become more secure no matter what your situation is. In fact, you can move toward secure if you're single, or even if you are currently in a relationship with an avoidant attacher. (It's just *A LOT* harder.)

So no matter your relationship status or how deeply anxious you are, take heart. There's hope of becoming more secure in love.

Secure attachment is truly the way to relational happiness. Think self-esteem! Think independence and autonomy! Think healthy intimate exchanges! The secure have resilience in the face of adversity, management of their reactions and feelings, and prosocial coping skills. Their friendships are better. They enjoy better relationships with friends, parents, and authority figures. They have better sex. There's high trust, intimacy, and affection as well as empathy, compassion, and awareness. What's not to love!?

You can get there. I believe just about anyone can... (avoidants, too!) And it may seem like a pipe dream right now, but people improve their attachment styles all the time with hard work. Get this; you're doing it just by reading this very book, so way to go!

Now, it's time to bust out your credit or library card. Your first homework assignment is here!

Homework/Reading Assignments

The surest path to changing your mind and behavior is education. We can't change what we don't know. Your first step to change is becoming more aware of your thoughts and the very best way to do this is by journaling.

- *Buy a blank journal.*

If you've never journaled before, that's not a problem! If you're a horrible writer, that's OK, too. You're not trying to write anything good, or clear, or even legible. You don't have to ever re-read what you write. The whole point is just slowing down and putting your thoughts and feelings down on paper, taking a moment to look at and digest the words. Take notes on what you're learning, or rip the pages out and burn them after you get your thoughts down. It's private, undirected, low-pressure, and inexpensive. Best of all, it *works*.

Grab an old notebook and pen, or buy a brand new journal. You can find The Anxious Hearts Journal on Amazon, full of prompts specifically written for Anxious Hearts, in case you need some more assistance. Now sit down and make your first journal entry today. Remember to add the date!

Write about whatever you like, but at some point focus on any strong emotions that you felt during your day. Explore any emotions, good or bad. What you felt, why you think the feeling came about, where and when you had the emotion. And remember, there are no wrong ways to do this.

Make a goal of writing daily, even if it's just a line or two. The ritual of taking a moment to reflect on your strong emotions will slowly make you more aware of when these emotions pop up. That awareness, over time, will pave the way for being able to better control them.

- *Take a quiz online and find out your attachment style.*

Suggested reading for this point in your journey

The books that I read at the very beginning of my journey were my springboard to change. They opened my eyes to new ways of thinking about my behavior and my relationships. These books all helped me to understand why I behaved as I did in my relationships. I wholeheartedly recommend the following books as wonderful "first steps" toward changing your attachment and relationships for the better.

Attached *by Amir Levine and Rachel Heller*[6]

For anyone interested in attachment theory, this is the gold standard. Attached is, in my opinion, the very best book out there regarding attachment theory. Regardless of your attachment style or background, this one is a must-read for anyone who wants to understand more about the topic.

Women Who Love Too Much *by Robin Norwood*[7]

As a woman who absolutely loved too much, too quickly, and often all the wrong people, this book was a game changer for me. I recommend it enthusiastically to friends who are struggling in unhappy relationships. This one opened my eyes to how my behavior was pushing away the people I loved.

---

6 Levine, A., & Heller, R. (2012). Attached: The New Science of Adult Attachment and How It Can Help You Find—and Keep—Love. Reprint edition. New York: TarcherPerigee.
7 Norwood, R. (2008). Women Who Love Too Much: When You Keep Wishing and Hoping He'll Change (1st ed.). New York: Pocket Books.

Insecure in Love, how Anxious Attachment Can Make You Feel Jealous, Needy, and Worried and What You Can Do About It
by Leslie Becker-Phelps[8]

After *Attached*, I'd say this book was probably the next most helpful in understanding why I would act the way I did in romantic relationships. Every page felt like a revelation. The author is incredibly knowledgeable about the behavior of anxious attachers and provides massive insight as well as exercises and ways out of this destructive mindset.

The Highly Sensitive Person in Love *by Elaine N. Aron*[9]

It shouldn't come as a surprise to you that a lot of anxious attachers are also highly sensitive people! This book contained page after page of advice on how individuals of intense emotions, high empathy, and high sensitivity experience and suffer in love.

Next, we're going to dive right into some big change. Your body, your mind, and the way that you relate to others will be the focus of Chapters 2 and 3. No matter what your circumstances or attachment style, many people struggle with self-esteem. Undoubtedly, a love and respect for yourself is the very foundation of relationship happiness, so building this foundation is the natural step after awareness.

---

8 Becker-Phelps, L. (2014). Insecure in Love: How Anxious Attachment Can Make You Feel Jealous, Needy, and Worried and What You Can Do About It (1st ed.). Oakland, CA: New Harbinger Publications.
9 Aron, E. (2009). The Highly Sensitive Person. New York: Harmony.

If you find yourself resistant at first, don't fret because that's perfectly normal! The process of building yourself up can be extremely uncomfortable but gets easier with practice and paves the way to the kind of life and love you want for yourself.

So what are you waiting for, Anxious Heart? Let's begin.

"IT'S NOT WHO YOU ARE THAT HOLDS YOU BACK, IT'S WHO YOU THINK YOU'RE NOT."

DENIS WAITLEY, MOTIVATIONAL SPEAKER

CHAPTER TWO

BUILDING SELF-WORTH

Do you feel worthy of love?

You might be taking a mental inventory of everything you've got going for you right now. Maybe you have a good job. Maybe you think your hair always looks cool. Math whiz? Awesome cook? Maybe you've got killer eyes and you know it. (Seriously! And it's not just your mom who tells you that!)

You may take in all of these things and think *Yeah, my self-esteem is alright.*

(Brace yourself, my friend, there's another truth bomb comin' at ya.)

If you're chasing love and trying to convince someone that you're worth their affection, your self-esteem is not alright...at all.

I say this because at the root of *every* insecurely attached individual is a deep-seated insecurity about their inherent lovability. Even if you consciously think, "I am worthy of being loved," your actions and behaviors might not support this thought.

When you ask yourself why partners have not been good to you in the past, consider this question: are *you* good to yourself? Perhaps they are following your example?

Do you find yourself constantly putting your needs aside for those of your partner/love interest? Do you constantly perform in ways that you hope will earn their love/respect? Do you find yourself begging/nagging them about not feeling loved? Do you fail to set aside time and energy to take care of your physical, mental, and emotional needs?

The way that you treat and conduct yourself is a much better indicator of your self-esteem.

One problem is that when we're sitting alone in our heads deciding if we're worthy of love, we're not thinking about our cool job or hairstyle or math skills. Sadly, it's not necessarily how much credit we give our good traits that decides whether or not we think we're worthy of the love of someone great. It's how much credit we give to the things we think *we're not*.

How many times have you faced the end of a relationship or unrequited love with thoughts like these:

If I were skinnier/in better shape they'd be more attracted to me.
I wish I wasn't so awkward. Then they'd see how funny I am and want to talk more.
If I were more successful, she'd respect me and treat me like a real prospect.
If I were beautiful like his ex then he'd commit to me.

We can torture ourselves all day long with thoughts of what we're not.

The secret of self-esteem and confidence is this: The only thing that really matters is how *you* feel about yourself regarding your current fitness/wit/financial stability/beauty. And if you don't feel good about it, you're going to act in ways that reflect this. These actions will shape the way that people treat you, further reinforcing your negative thoughts about yourself.

This concept can be a little tough to wrap your brain around, but bear with me. It's kind of like the emperor's invisible clothes; if you think that you look fantastic, others are more likely to, as well. Even better, if you're truly satisfied with what you've got, you won't care about the haters anyway. Gone will be the desire to impress anyone and you'll glow with the satisfaction and confidence that draws great partners like moths to a flame.

Easier said than done, I know.

To complicate things further, sometimes we can tell ourselves, *"I'm a great person!"* while simultaneously wondering, *"Why am I not enough?"*

So how does one go about building the kind of self-esteem that others can *see* and we can *feel*? It's not easy. It takes a lot of hard work across a few different important categories. We're actually going to spend the next two chapters discussing how to improve your physical, mental, and relational confidence. That's because there's another term you might have seen floating around: *self-worth*. Self-worth is the belief that you are loveable and valuable regardless of how you evaluate your traits; it is the glorious result of the hard work of building our self-esteem.

And with self-worth, you can become your own best advocate in any relationship; romantic or otherwise.

No time to waste—let's get on with it.

Physical Self-Esteem

I know, I know.

Not another person telling me that I need to get into shape!

But I've got a bit of a twist on the traditional "get into shape" spiel: this time, there's no goal.

This is because there's no magical number on the scale, no amount of weight that you can bench press or superhuman speed you can run a mile in that will guarantee someone's love. Now, don't get me wrong, it's not that these things don't help people notice us. Of course they do. It's hard not to notice someone in fantastic shape zipping past as they crush their 10-mile run without breaking a sweat. Being in amazing shape is very appealing— it's true.

But, seriously? No goal?

Nope. I don't care how much weight you lose, lift, or keep on you. And why is that? It's for the same reason that diets don't work.

There's a huge difference between extrinsic motivation (wanting to do something because of something outside of yourself) and intrinsic motivation (wanting to do something because you truly want it for yourself). Only one of these works long-term. (Hint: it's not the one where you find yourself trying to get in shape for someone else's approval...)

If you are only working out for the purpose of attracting someone's admiration or attention, guess what happens the second you lock them down? That's right; you go right back to the couch. Working out for the sole purpose of attracting someone special does not raise your self-esteem in any permanent, sustainable way.

You might think that the absence of a goal means that you're not going to achieve anything. This might not be the instant-gratification, satisfying "get-rich-quick" kind of plan that promises that you'll hit your goal weight "in six months or your money back, guaranteed!" Truly, you might not hit your goal weight, or do a pull-up, or be able to bench record-breaking amounts of weight. The reward, surprisingly, is in *the process*. When you make a goal of consistently showing yourself that your health matters to you every single day for six months, at the end of that period, you've spent six months proving to yourself with daily action that you matter. You've established a habit of taking care of yourself that sets a new standard for how you treat your body. You've put some of your valuable, finite energy into taking care of yourself and working toward the best you that you can be.

And that, friend, is where real, unshakable, undeniable self-esteem is born. It doesn't come from giant, bulging muscles or super low numbers on the scale. Self-esteem is simply an attitude about how you treat yourself and what you feel like you deserve—regardless of any physical feats you're capable of. It means that you can be overweight and still be attractive. It means that you don't have to lift more than any guy in the room and someone will still think you're strong. It means that you can have the slowest mile of anyone at your gym and someone will still admire the drive and effort you put forth to make that run every single day. (Psst! That someone is *you!*) And that is very good news, indeed.

There are no magical numbers to strive for, there are no concrete quali-fications in order for someone to love your body, and the kind of self-esteem that you envy in confident, self-loving folks is extraordinarily achievable.

We're working to remove this unhelpful thought: *I am not in good shape.* And replace it with something much healthier: *I am the kind of person who dedicates part of every day to taking care of my physical health because my body and health are important to me.*

Make a Plan

To be sure, there are thousands of guides on how to lose weight or cre-ate a healthier lifestyle for yourself. I don't need to waste any words telling you exactly how to go about that. Instead, I'm going to touch on some ideas that these weight loss, extreme-diet, alternative-lifestyle books might not.

Consider Fun Over Serious Fat Burning

New routines can be incredibly tough to implement. Make things easier on yourself by choosing something active that you love, or at least some-thing that you could grow to love. Once, with nothing but the best inten-tions, I purchased a very nice, very expensive treadmill. I set up a routine for running and marked my accomplishments every day on the calendar…and found myself, one month later, wiping the thin layer of dust off the machine (which had quickly transformed into the most expensive clothes hanger I'd ever purchased). No matter how great my intentions were or how much money I had spent, I couldn't ignore the fact that I simply hated running on a treadmill and would probably never be able to make a sustainable habit out of it.

Mere months after my failed treadmill experience, I went for a walk outside on a sunny afternoon. It was so nice and relaxing that I decided to do it again the next day. And the next. And before I knew it, I had formed a new exercise habit. Sure, you've got to walk pretty far to burn the kind of calories you would on a run. But as the months wore on, those walks added up. I noticed that I was slowly getting into quite good shape! It just goes to show that a less intense exercise routine that you love is going to be a lot more effective than something hardcore that you know you don't enjoy.

Consider Trying Something New

On the other side of the coin, I was once convinced to join a very intense gym. I had never done any kind of weight training before and hated cardio with a passion; this gym combined both on the daily. But to my surprise, the camaraderie and energy of the gym regulars was tough to resist. Friendly faces and fun conversation greeted me every time I walked in the doors. In no time at all, I found myself attending classes almost daily, without charts or stickers or any incentive at all beyond the fact that I really enjoyed going. The friendships I found at the gym began to spill over beyond class time. And even better, I found myself unexpectedly and unintentionally in the best shape of my life. But perhaps best of all, I had formed a habit of regular exercise that continues to this day.

Consider Strength Training

There's something about strength training—working to make your body stronger and achieve higher goals—that tends to spill over into the rest of your headspace and makes you mentally stronger, too. I know I don't need to sell the guys on this one! Men dream of having bigger muscles as soon as they are old enough to have dreams. But ladies, hear me out. I am a very short, petite, and rather nerdy woman. There's no universe where I would have imagined (let alone dreamed) that one day strength training would make me feel more confident, youthful-looking, energetic, and attractive than I'd ever imagined I could be. Consider thinking outside the treadmill and elliptical routine when you consider ways that you might enjoy getting active.

Consider Getting Social with It

Don't hate me, introverts! Group activities that you join are likely going to be 1) more of a commitment; 2) more fun; and 3) make your life more full and enjoyable than any solo activity you choose. Sports teams (i.e. intramural volleyball, a local softball or bowling league, or even a neighborhood jogging group) can boost your social life as well as provide an incredible sense of accomplishment (think tournaments, wins, and marathons!). As long as the whole point of our fitness journey is to boost our self-esteem, this seems like a big no-brainer bonus. Pick a sport/activity, find your people, and start enjoying those personal wins. And if you're terribly introverted and just fine with that, feel free to ignore this one!

Go Ahead, Play to Your Strengths

Were you always an amazing swimmer as a child? Maybe hit the pool and see how it feels getting back into it. Did you have a great sense of balance but never joined gymnastics? Maybe you've always been flexible. Have you ever tried yoga? There are adult classes for just about every sport you can think of. You know yourself best! What are you good at? Your fitness journey is about much more than weight loss. When your goal is to get the most bang for your buck in your brain, now is a great time to tip the scales in your favor and pick something that you know you can crush.

Whatever you do to get yourself moving is a good choice. Don't worry if you don't see yourself losing weight or finally revealing the six-pack that you always hoped was hiding under there...the habit of regularly taking care of your body and showing yourself that love and consideration is what we're looking for.

Making time to work on your body also conveys a high level of self-worth and self-respect (even if you don't have that attidude yet!) and is very appealing to anyone you might be interested in dating. If we show others that we care about ourselves and our bodies, it communicates to them how they should treat us too.

Above all, consistency is key. Show yourself (and your body) love every single day until it becomes more natural.

A love and respect for our body lays a great foundation for the even tougher job ahead: cultivating love and respect for our brain.

Mental Self-esteem

Ah, the task of improving mental self-esteem. This is another topic that entire sections of libraries are dedicated to. At its heart, this book is one of them! It's a very popular topic. Trust me when I say that you're far from alone in wondering:

What's wrong with me? Why can't I just make my brain do what it's supposed to?

And even as someone who makes it a point to read a book or two per month on this stuff, I can say without a doubt that no book I ever read helped me as much as therapy. The single most important thing I ever did for my mental health was to book an appointment with a mental health professional.

The thing is, you could be the most self-aware person around. You might, like me, absolutely love reading and have no problem devouring books on all the topics that you struggle with. You might have a super enlightened friend who gives you amazing advice. Maybe your partner is an A+ listener. It's also possible that you've been journaling for a while now and feel like you've already figured yourself out.

But really, truly, sometimes we're just too close to the topic to see ourselves as clearly as an outside party who just so happens to have an advanced degree on the brain and human behavior.

It's pure pride that allows us to think that we could do as good a job of figuring our baggage out as the professionals. And maybe it's fear that makes us think that they might not do a good job. You might have had a bad experience in couples therapy or with a professional who wasn't a good match for you. Whatever your objections, consider this suggestion with an open mind.

We don't hesitate to visit a doctor when we are ill. If our brains are causing serious unrest in our lives a mental health professional is the person best equipped to help you get things back on track.

So how do you go about choosing one?

Make a Plan

If you've never gone to therapy before (or if you had a negative experience in the past) finding a therapist can be daunting. There's a lot to consider and many different options, so I'll try to break things down to make the process as easy and painless as possible.

After all, the hard work should be done on your therapist's cozy couch…not worrying about how to go about getting yourself there!

The first, most pressing thing to consider is cost. It probably won't shock you to hear that therapy can be incredibly expensive. An uninsured person visiting a private therapist can easily pay between $65 and $250 per hour (or more)! But don't let this dishearten you; there are many other options.

If you're uninsured, there are student health centers at local colleges/universities as well as federally qualified community based health centers that provide free or low-cost mental health services, often on a sliding payment scale basis. The counselors and therapists-in-training at universities are able to provide their services at a much-reduced cost while they earn their certifications.

Nonprofit organizations sometimes offer therapy at lower cost to the public. Your employer may also have a program in place that offers therapy to employees free of charge. Check with your human resources department to find out. Another little known fact is that many private therapists are willing to negotiate their rates or give clients a discount if they can pay in cash. (Hey, it never hurts to ask!)

In recent years, many inexpensive online therapy options have popped up. There are therapists who will video chat, therapists who will communicate with you completely over text message, therapists who are available digitally 24/7, and even some who just correspond by email. For anyone hesitant (or financially unable) to attend traditional therapy, these can be wonderful options.

For the insured, your first step will be checking with your insurance on who your in-network therapists are. You can make a phone call to your insurance company or log on to your insurance provider's website for a list of names and numbers. Your visit to an in-network therapist might be partially or completely covered depending on your level of insurance coverage.

Next, make a list of therapists' names and numbers (or attractive online therapy services) and start doing your research.

You can call therapists and ask them about themselves, or type their names into Google and search on your own terms. Here are a few questions to consider:

- *What are their certifications?*

Get to know the letters following a therapist's name and what they mean. Whether they are a psychiatrist, psychologist, professional counselor, or clinical social worker, different types of mental health professionals have different focuses and treatments. A little research here goes a long way.

- *What are their specialties?*

Many therapists list their specialties online. Are you looking for a therapist who has a lot of experience in LGBTQ+ relationships? Someone whose focus is on depression, anxiety, bipolar, or other mental illnesses? A therapist's specialties and concentrations can tell you a lot about them before you ever pick up the phone. Pay attention to these and find what speaks to you.

- *What is important to you?*

Do you feel much more comfortable talking to someone the same gender as you? Maybe an opposite gender therapist would be more your style? Are you opposed to the idea of driving very far for therapy? Don't forget to consider a therapist's availability; does their schedule work with yours? These are all big considerations and wonderful questions for that initial phone call to see if you'd like to set up an appointment.

Here are more questions that you can pose to prospective therapists:

- How long have you been working as a counselor/therapist?
- How much experience do you have working with people who are struggling with what I have described? And how well does therapy seem to work for them?
- What kind of treatments do you usually recommend/implement? (e.g. medication, cognitive behavioral therapy, homework, etc.) and how do they work?
- How long do you typically see someone for? How do we assess whether or not it's working for me? What do we do if this doesn't work?

When you've identified a therapist or two (or three) who you think might be a good fit, schedule your first appointment with them. Often therapists will see new patients free of charge to determine if the fit is right, and many others will provide this initial appointment at a reduced cost.

So what are you looking for in that initial appointment?

Therapy can be incredibly uncomfortable. It can mean sharing things you've never told anyone before, things that are scary to discuss that can bring up intense, overwhelming emotions. With that in mind, you want to find someone who you feel comfortable talking to. Choose someone whom you feel a good rapport with—a feeling of connection and engagement when you're talking to them is great. They should feel kind, understanding, and non-judgmental. If any of those are missing, this may not be your best therapist.

In my own search, I interviewed a couple of different therapists who—while being perfectly nice, intelligent, and qualified—I simply did not feel a connection with. I politely declined further sessions and they were gracious and understanding (after all, it's part of their job!). The therapist I ultimately chose made me feel instantly comfortable. We were able to laugh and joke often during my sessions, which went a long way to ease my nerves. We were also able to dive into topics that brought up big feelings of anger, shame, and sadness for me. No matter what we covered in our sessions, every time I walked in I truly felt like I was in the company of a good friend.

One more thing to consider is choosing someone who challenges you. Therapy is not just about having someone smiling, nodding, and endlessly validating everything you tell them. Your therapist should make you think! *Why are you thinking/acting/feeling the way you are? Is this how you want to feel/be/remain?* They might even make you work! The weekly homework challenges that my therapist gave me were often quite difficult and pushed me outside of my comfort zone in ways that brought about massive growth for me.

Even still, years after my last appointment, I can imagine his gentle, guiding voice in my head when I'm faced with an emotional dilemma. My experiences in his office have stayed with me and continue to help guide me in my life going forward! For me, it was money well spent.

Your experience in therapy will be determined by a few different factors: 1) how well matched you are with your therapist, 2) how open you are to the process and the information that your therapist has for you, and 3) how willing you are to *do the work*. The work of therapy is what happens after your therapist opens your eyes to the reasons behind your struggles. Do you sink further in your convictions that you're damaged and that the world is out to get you? Or do you take that information and say *What can I do with this? How can I use this information to make my life better?*

The outcome of therapy is entirely up to you. Remember, it won't always be easy, but it will always be worth it. And remember that it's not easy to work on our mental health. You're very brave to even consider the undertaking!

Anxious Heart, give yourself time. Give yourself credit. Accept that there *will* be hard days and keep on working.

OK! So you're working on your physical self-esteem. That's great! Hopefully, you're also now researching therapists to start diving in on your mental health too. But in the meantime, you're still going to be running into situations that need to be handled.

You know, as an insecure attacher, that these daily situations are the crux of your struggles. Whether you're struggling with what to say or do when confronted with relationship problems or difficult dating scenarios, taking the wrong steps or making a bad choice, or simply riding the rough emotional waves that come with love, real life can come at you fast.

While on your journey, I have a secret weapon for you. Read on. I want you to be armed with this tool *during* your periods of great growth.

Mindfulness (Pause and Respond)

If one trait could be identified that seems to cause the most trouble for the insecurely attached, I think it would be our tendency to be highly reactive. Many stumble through life, finding themselves blindly reacting to whatever comes their way. They allow their unconscious mind to decide how they will think/act/feel and take immediate, often extreme actions that correspond in intensity with the feeling that preceded it.

Sure. You say. *Something happens to me and then I react to it. Isn't that just how brains work?*

Well, it doesn't have to be.

Where our significant others are involved, we insecurely attached folks can be especially volatile in our reactions. If you are anything like I used to be, the quality of your day is practically determined by the words or actions of the one you love. Are they in a crappy mood? You're going to be in one, too. A curt tone or rude comment can derail you and swiftly bring you down. Or alternatively, are they depressed? You're suddenly a ray of sunshine working like crazy to cheer them up. The insecurely attached person is not in control of their day or mood or well-being. They are stuck in a boat adrift on the sea of their significant other's mood, hoping for calm waters but feeling completely thrown about by whatever emotional storms arise. Although this may seem natural to you (well of course, why wouldn't I feel affected by my significant other's mood!?) it is not necessarily healthy.

It's one thing to be attuned to your beloved's mood. It's kind to be sensitive to their needs, even loving to feel great empathy or have a desire to lift them up. But it's another thing entirely to be personally at the mercy of their changing moods. This is one of the hallmarks of codependency; an unhealthy, excessive emotional or psychological reliance on a partner. If we are susceptible to absorbing or trying to change every mood that strikes them, eventually they may begin hiding their moods from us. After all, who could safely experience the occasional gloomy afternoon knowing that they'll be pulling the one they love down with them? And how comfortable would you be expressing negative emotions knowing that your partner is deeply disturbed by your bad mood and will work relentlessly to change it?

Emotions (even negative ones!) need to be okay for everyone to have from time to time. And it's also vital that within a relationship, these emotions are not quite so contagious. Our partners need us to be rocks for them, something steady that they can hold onto when tough emotions assail them.

But how do we allow others to have their bad moods without it bombing our day? How do we start thinking of ourselves as strong, confident, unshakable rocks that our significant others can rely and depend on, rather than someone they have to tiptoe around?

There is a concept that you may have heard of called *mindfulness* that can change the course of how you navigate your day-to-day life, giving you a lot more control over how you respond to your world—partner/love interest included. Mindfulness is a focus and awareness of the present moment. It is the calm acknowledgment and acceptance of everything that one is sensing, thinking, and feeling. It doesn't mean that you enjoy these feelings or observations, just that you notice them and are aware of them. While that doesn't seem like the kind of thing that can change your circumstances, it is deceptively powerful.

Most people are floating along in life letting their senses, thoughts, and emotions make decisions for them. Discomfort, upsets, preconditioned ways of thinking, fears—we let these things drive our words and actions daily at the cost of our happiness and relationships. The very first step toward not being controlled by the sensations that pass through our minds is simply noticing them and naming them.

Step 1. Become aware of your senses/thoughts/feelings by labelling them.

When we're aware of the thought or feeling, we have much more control over how we'd like to deal with it. Are you feeling angry? What does that feel like? Is it a heat rising in your cheeks? A pressure in your mind that boils hotter and hotter as moments pass? Is it a trembling feeling of injustice way down in your gut? Or maybe you're feeling depressed? Perhaps the colors and sounds you're used to aren't as bright? These feelings that you notice can be *good,* too. Perhaps it's your birthday and you're carrying a buzzing excitement in your chest all day because you know a wonderful gift is heading your way in the evening?

The insecurely attached are often tragically bad at noticing/labeling our feelings because we work so hard to avoid them. Unfortunately, avoiding them means that we don't know what we're feeling. And if we don't know what we're feeling, we can be inadvertently controlled by our emotions. Your actions and words are shaped by these feelings whether you realize it or not.

And without awareness, our actions can be shaped by our feelings in ways that we might not like. Those thoughts and feelings have ways of flavoring everything that we put out into the world. They can leak out into our relationships even when we think we're hiding them well. Awareness and acknowledgment, then, is a logical first step.

When we're aware of the thought or feeling, we have much more control over how we'd like to deal with it.

When your body begins to feel different, disturbed, or otherwise changed from a calm, neutral state, take note. Try to put a label on the sensations that arise. If you're able, sit with the feeling and try to really experience it; that can also help you identify it.

Step 2. The Pause.

When you become aware of a sensation/thought/feeling the next step is to utilize *The Pause*. The Pause is, I believe, the most powerful step.

The moment that we become aware of a sensation/thought/feeling, we are not yet ready to decide our next move because our bodies and minds are activated, fully involved with whatever we're experiencing. Let me explain what I mean by that. Imagine that your date or significant other calls to tell you that they need to cancel your evening plans: *"I'm sorry, I have to cancel. Something just came up last minute. Is that OK?"* Immediately, without having to think, you're going to feel a certain way in response to that news. It might feel like a heat in your chest or a tightness in your throat. I've often been aware of a sinking feeling in my stomach when receiving news of this sort. That feeling is going to flavor how you answer them, whether you realize what you're feeling or not.

This is where The Pause comes in. When you're feeling activated (disappointed, angry, surprised, anxious, upset, nervous, uncomfortable, excited, etc.) *you don't have to answer or act right away.*

People who struggle with insecure attachment can be very reactionary and tend to think/act negatively as soon as that stimulus hits them.

Resist this urge! You don't have to jump as soon as a feeling arises.

Upsetting stimuli (especially coming from the object of your affection) can set off an irresistible desire to get closer to them. (For avoidant attachers, the reaction will be that of needing more space.) Neither of these reactions are inherently *bad*, but they can definitely be problematic if taken too far and can be greatly upsetting to your partner.

Before you say or do anything, give yourself a moment to come down from that heightened, reactionary state. It may take moments or it may take hours or days. If someone is waiting for your answer/response, you can let them know that you'd like a little bit of time to process what they said before you answer. Unless it's an emergency, they will most likely be glad that you're treating what they said seriously. At the very least, they will respect that you are having strong emotions and would like to calm down before you make any decisions.

Whether it takes just a moment or an entire day to start feeling more like your normal self, your return to a calm state will be a godsend in facilitating a healthy follow-up conversation. However long it takes, the most important thing is that you feel calm and rational before you determine your next move.

Step 3. Respond instead of React.

Now we're going to use our calm state to *respond* instead of react. These may sound like the same thing. Far from it, my friend; they're very different!

In *reaction*, there's no choice. Break the word down! Re-act. We are acted upon and in return we act in a similar, reciprocal fashion. There's no thinking with reaction; it's automatic and unplanned. When we allow ourselves to react without thought we are operating blindly based on our sensations/thoughts/feelings that we likely haven't acknowledged. This isn't how we want to live, is it? Imagine yourself forever on autopilot, letting the primitive parts of your brain dictate how you go about your day and conduct your relationships. No, surely we can do better than that.

Remember your hypothetical date who had something "come up last minute"? Without thinking, you may have felt disrespected, dismissed, unimportant, unloved, angry, or maybe even felt a desire for revenge. A knee-jerk reaction to them flaking out on your plans might sound like this:

Them: *"I'm sorry, I have to cancel. Something just came up. Is that OK?"*
You: *"No! It isn't okay! I cleared my Friday night and made reservations for us and now you're just cancelling at the last minute? You're such a selfish jerk!"*

Oof. That didn't go so well, did it?

Or, worse: *"Yeah, that's totally OK. Let me know when you'll be free! :-)"*

This answer is fine if you really didn't mind, but if it's not really OK and you know you'll be spending the next few days feeling lousy about it, this response is a first class ticket to resentment.

The healthier way would be to *respond*. A response requires thought, reflection, and choice. When you receive some sort of stimulus, utilize The Pause, during which you can ask yourself awesome questions like, "How do I want to respond to this? What sort of person do I want to be? What would feel best for me?"

Now, let's look at your flaky date again.

"I'm sorry, I have to cancel. Something just came up. Is that OK?"

Take a deep breath, collect your thoughts, and try to place yourself in their shoes. Maybe they are suffering from sudden digestive issues and they're too embarrassed to say so? Perhaps they have a family emergency? No matter what the issue, you can use this space to decide what type of person you want to be. Do you want to be the type who flies off the handle and gets upset when they feel disappointed? Certainly not! Especially considering that your date may have a legitimate issue that prompted them to cancel.

One more deep breath, and then a kind, self-respectful response might sound like this:

"Things happen, I understand. I do feel disappointed, though. I cleared my Friday night for this and I was really looking forward to going out with you. I would appreciate a little bit more heads-up in the future so I can schedule something else if need be. Let me know when you're free next and I would love to reschedule."

Empathy on point. Dignity preserved. Healthy boundaries for the future set. Door left open (or at least ajar!) for the possibility of future connection. I know, this kind of response is much easier said than done and takes loads of practice. But we'll get to that!

For now, this method (Mindfulness. The Pause. Respond rather than React.) is a fantastic tool that will help you in all your future relationship interactions. Even if you don't end up sending the perfect response chock-full of healthy boundaries and confidence, your response is bound to be better if preceded by a big pause, some time to calm down, and reflection on how you'd like to respond to the situation.

Identifying Your Crazy

We can all feel a little bit crazy at times. Even your most stable, even-keeled friend has moments that make them feel a little unhinged. The most important difference between dysfunctional and functional crazy is *awareness*. Do you believe and act on all of the upsetting things that pop into your brain? Do you follow those wild, upsetting impulses? Or do you recognize that strong emotions and impulses are simply feelings that will pass and don't need to be acted upon? It's an important part of your journey that you spend time looking at your crazy.

An impulse that anxious attachers have is an unhealthy focus on others—what they say, what they think, what they do. Are you an anxious attacher who is hyper-focused on how you can put yourself in everyone else's favor?

Redirect your focus inward. This time of analyzing your mind may be turbulent. The discomfort you may feel diving into your own mind is normal but can be quite uncomfortable. Prepare yourself for some sleepless nights as you begin to confront your demons.

But what do we do if we're so close to our troubles that we can't see them clearly? What do we do when we're unable to come up with a coherent reason why others seem to push our love away? (Or we push away the love of others?) This inability to step outside of ourselves leaves us confused, confounded, lying awake wondering endlessly: *What's wrong with me?*

The answer often lies in our shadow.

One of the late, great founding fathers of modern psychology, Carl Jung, defined our shadow as the unknown, dark side of our personality. It is a place we typically forbid our conscious minds to go; confronting it can be painful, scary, or just plain difficult. It is the place in our minds where we know where we fall short or need work, but rather than acknowledge and work on this, we tend to project that (and the disapproval of it) onto other people.

If you took my suggestion in Chapter 1 and bought yourself a journal, pull it out now. If you didn't, you can still play along. Name a couple of very positive traits that define you! Quick, don't think too hard about it! (I consider my optimism and empathy to be a couple of my most defining positive characteristics.)

Now, write down what the opposite of those things are. These are probably traits that you *absolutely can't stand* in other people. (For me, if someone is pessimistic and/or refuses to see things from another person's perspective, I can't handle it!) There's your shadow. It's the opposite of what you value, the things that we can't tolerate in others and certainly can't tolerate in ourselves. Yet, these traits exist in us to some degree no matter how hard we try to deny them. We can expend quite a bit of energy trying to avoid them. Sometimes we can even try *too hard* to avoid our shadows. This overcompensation can cause all kinds of trouble in our lives. Surprisingly, this may even be your *biggest* trouble. Don't worry if this one leaves your head spinning. This is some deep stuff!

And truly, shadow work and exploration is often better left to the professionals. This is territory best traveled with a kind, knowledgeable guide in the form of a trusted therapist. But there are some easier, important questions you can ask yourself to start down a path of self-reflection, betterment, and shining a light on your shadow.

- What kind of things in my life are causing me to struggle? Are these needs that I can't seem to get met? Are they things that I seem to be missing or unable to accomplish? Is it an emotion that I'm having trouble grappling with like anger, frustration, or resentment?
- What situations do I find myself in when my struggles appear? Are there locations where I find myself feeling like this often? (Work, home, the bedroom, out on dates, etc.)

- In what ways might I contribute to my struggles? Am I putting myself in uncomfortable situations over and over again without changing anything? Am I unknowingly provoking attacks? Am I avoiding dealing with someone/something in such a way that it continues to be a problem?
- How would my life look if this wasn't a problem anymore? Is there anything healthy that I can do that might help me work toward getting closer to this goal?

Of course, I don't expect anyone to be their own counselor! But this is a great thought experiment to get yourself focusing on the ways that you can control and better your own situation. Start becoming aware of how you act and feel within relationships that are important to you. Are you experiencing a lot of stress or anxiety around someone you love? How do you feel about your actions around this person? Start asking yourself questions and answering honestly: *How do I feel?*

For the first six months of my journaling, I was simply recording things that were hard to deal with. Situations that made me angry, sad, or uncomfortable. They were all written down along with the places where they occurred, my reactions that I wasn't happy with, and how I wished things could have been instead.

While I did not see a lot of growth or change during this time, the exercise did help me get much better at recognizing my crazy. In time, I was able to predict when situations that might appear in my journal were about to occur and I could find my way out of them or at the very least, mentally prepare myself before they started getting tough.

Anxious attachers tend to use other people (especially their romantic partners or love interests) to regulate their emotions. This is not only extremely unhealthy, but feels terrible to experience. In this position, we find ourselves completely at the mercy of someone else to calm us, pacify our upsets, and make us happy. We are essentially adrift on their ocean. Their storms will shake us and their calm will soothe us. When we allow others to dictate how we feel, we have effectively given up control over our own emotional state.

The anxious attacher is freed only when they can learn to emotionally regulate themselves and stop over-relying on others.

So how can we self-regulate and stop straining our relationships in this way?

- Spending time in nature
- Listening to music that matches or improves our mood
- Deep breathing
- Reading
- Exercise
- Meditation
- Journaling

This list is far from exhaustive. Anything that takes your mind off of anxieties and calms/energizes your heart can pull you out of an uncomfortable, dysregulated state. One of my favorite ways to self-regulate when I'm feeling wound up is to hit up my local rock climbing gym. It's almost impossible for me to worry or ruminate when I'm hanging onto the wall, focusing on where my hands and feet will go next. Then, when I feel better, I am able to think more clearly about whatever it was that upset me. When we are able to calm ourselves and make our own happiness, we are truly in control. Our ability to self-regulate also frees up our partners to come closer to us; they stop feeling overburdened when they are no longer alone in managing our emotions.

Work on recognizing when you are turning to a partner before you attempt to calm/soothe/reassure yourself. If we want things to change, we've got to stop operating on autopilot and start recognizing when we're engaging in unhealthy coping mechanisms. Be gentle with yourself! That takes time and a lot of practice.

You Don't Have to Be Perfect to Be Loved

Let me be the first person to tell you:

Your anxiety is lying to you.

It sounds so convincing, so persuasive. But that voice in your head whispering all of your darkest fears, predicting a terrible future that must be avoided at all costs…it's not to be trusted. Now, don't get me wrong. It's *vital* that we pay attention to what makes us feel anxious and listen to our bodies about what we need. But it's equally important that we don't believe everything that our anxious voice is telling us.

When attachment anxiety kicks in, the dark words, thoughts, and feelings that keep repeating in your mind may feel true. However, it's more likely your activated alarm system (set in place when you were a child for good reason) and not a good indicator of the future or the truth. When you let these thoughts influence your thoughts and behavior it can prevent you from finding the healthy relationship that you want.

I have spent many sleepless nights with disturbing thoughts racing through my mind. Most of them were centered on love (or a lack of it) and I wondered when I would ever be "enough" to be loved. This will sound familiar to the insecurely attached.

A deep-seated feeling that you're not worthy of love is the culprit here. Insecure attachers tend to have the unfortunate trait of holding a deep, unsettling belief that they are inherently unlovable. We believe that if we were to be *truly* seen and known, we would be rejected. And if we don't feel like we're lovable or worthy of love, we will seek out others who treat us that way and affirm our belief. This is why it's so important to build up your self-esteem before you put your heart out on the line again.

Contrary to what your brain is telling you, *you don't have to be perfect to be loved.* You are actually lovable right now, as is, without any improvement at all. But without self-awareness, self-work, and efforts to curb our problematic and toxic relationship behaviors, we're going to end up pushing away anyone who is trying to love us in spite of our flaws.

A belief that we are unlovable can also lead to people pleasing behavior. This is when we mold ourselves to be exactly what we think others want, strive to always be available, have trouble setting healthy boundaries, and are willing to do whatever it takes to make others happy or gain their approval. Unfortunately, living as this extra-helpful façade as opposed to being true to ourselves further cements the belief that who we *really* are deep down isn't worthy of being loved.

So what are some actionable things you can do to make yourself actually believe that someone could love you for you, and not the fake representative that you're sending in your place?

1. Baby steps! Practice throwing out little bits of the real you. Pay attention when your friends/family show you love and acceptance.

Are you showing up as your authentic self? Or are you sending a fake representative who you think would be more pleasing in your place?

When I started my journey, I didn't have a significant other to practice on. But I knew that I needed to start work on being really genuine and feeling loved for it. My idea was to throw out little bits of the real me (say something nerdy, or silly, or vulnerable) and pay attention to the reaction from people who I knew were safe to experiment with. Typically, we breeze past and do not notice when our weirdness is accepted. But paying close attention to the ways that people respond positively to our "less appealing" qualities is a fantastic self-esteem builder.

2. Dive in! Get familiar with what you love. Get good at it.

It's easy to feel insecure about our abilities. It's even easier to feel embarrassed about them if they're unusual, strange, or even controversial! Add some bonus shame on top if you're not even particularly good at what you love. To that, I say dive in! Pursue the things that you love with zeal and then practice them to your heart's content until it's something you know back and forth, up and down, and can do with your eyes closed. Real passion and skill are extremely tough to hide and others will admire your enthusiasm. You may even start to admire it, too!

3. Embrace your weirdness.

That quirky, crazy "you-ness" that differentiates you from other people is the very thing that sets you apart in a vast sea of potential partners. You might think that your love of genealogy or that loud snort-laugh thing you do when a joke takes you by surprise will send people running for the hills. Surprisingly, it's just the opposite. Our quirks and weirdness have an unexpected appeal that we don't give nearly enough credit to.

4. Birds of a feather...surround yourself with people who care about your passions, accept you, and build you up.

Being accepted for the things that you love or the ways that you are is extremely validating. If we spend all of our time in crowds that tear us down for the strange things that we love, we inevitably start to feel unlovable. It's important that we spend lots of time with people who make us feel like we're awesome. Surround yourself with people who accept you and the things you love and you'll notice how *you* begin to accept you, too. Without doing the work toward loving and accepting yourself, you're simply making it more difficult for people to love you.

The things that you don't work on will push away even the strongest, best candidates who would like to love you. And that's another reason why it's so important to figure this stuff out. Sometimes people really want to love you but your unaddressed baggage piles up like an obstacle course and they can't get through. You don't have to be like this. By extending self-love and forgiveness to yourself and committing to doing the hard work, you're going to change the way you treat yourself. That will change the way others relate to you.

Say the following out loud, or write it down in your journal:

"I want to be gentle with myself and my progress even when it's hard and I feel like I've failed; maybe especially then. I want to see myself in the best light; the light that I view the ones I love in. I am working to make my life better and I am lovable, as I am right now, flaws and all."

It may feel like you don't mean it. Maybe you don't mean it yet! When I first wrote those sentences down in my journal, I didn't believe a word of them. Years later, I was thumbing through my old journals and found it again. To my delight, I realized that with all my hard work, I had created a new mindset in which all of those sentences rang true. It took years and hard work, but I made it. And if someone as anxiously attached as me can pull myself out of it, I believe that you can, too.

If you're still reading, you can be proud of that. This work is difficult and takes perseverance. Hopefully, we uncovered some big things for you in this chapter and you're feeling ready to dive in to round two of your homework and reading assignments.

Homework/Reading Assignments

- *Commit to a physical routine that you love.*

On your mission to change your self-esteem, you need to develop habits of self-love. Fitness is your first task; more specifically, creating a habit of respecting your body. Ideally, this should be something you enjoy that you can do daily. At the less physical end, committing to a ten-minute meditation break where you clear your thoughts, practice positive affirmation, or simply listen to relaxing music with your eyes closed is an effective, easy way to show yourself love, and respect your body every day. I do hope that you've also found a sport or physical activity that you can't wait to start. (Bonus points if it's a social one!)

Create a calendar to keep yourself accountable and make sure that you practice every day. And as I said before, the most important thing is that you're excited about this activity. It should be something that you look forward to. It should also be easy to do daily or weekly because it's fun and engaging. Even better if it's social and gets you out amongst (new!?) friends.

- *Ask your five closest friends to describe you in three positive words.*

For me, this experiment was both eye-opening and powerful.

I had absolutely no idea which words my friends would use to describe me. Because of this, I went into this experiment blind. Each answer I collected felt like a giant, surprise hug. Not only were my friends enthusiastic about thinking up the words to describe me, but I was genuinely touched by the thoughtfulness and sincerity with which they delivered their answers.

I was also pleasantly surprised to see the same words popping up from different friends.

Even now, years after I did this, I can remember what an incredible boost to my self-esteem this experiment was.

Remember to grab your journal and record their answers. Sometimes when I'm flipping through my old journal pages, I stumble upon that entry and the feeling of love and appreciation for my friends comes rushing back.

Know, as you record these answers, that friendships can be a wonderful way to work on our self-esteem when we're struggling.

• *Find a 21-Day Challenge to commit to.*

A 21-Day challenge offers three weeks of daily effort to change an aspect of your life that you'd like to change. This is about how much time it takes to form a new habit, but even if you're not going for long-term change here, you'd be surprised how much you can accomplish in three weeks of concerted effort.

On the next page, I've listed the 21-Day Challenge that I took early on my journey. I recognized my need for a self-esteem boost and found this highly-reviewed book very helpful.

However, if you're looking for a challenge specifically for anxious attachers, I've also created the 21-Day Anxious Attachment Challenge, available on Amazon. It contains three weeks worth of daily thoughts and challenges to help an anxious attacher move toward secure attachment. (It also closely follows the narrative arch of this book!)

Suggested reading for this point in your journey

The 21-Day Self-Love Challenge *by Ingrid Lindberg[10]*

I just love short, concentrated challenges like this. If you're struggling with self-esteem at all or even if you'd just like some prompts to beef up a regular routine of showing yourself love, this book does the trick. With a fun, accessible tone, and simple daily challenges, I guarantee you'll come out of this one feeling more lovable than you went in.

The Mindful Path to Self-Compassion: Freeing Yourself from Destructive Thoughts and Emotions *by Christopher K. Germer[11]*

As far as work on self-esteem goes, I would consider this book "pulling out the big guns." One of the most damaging things we do is feed ourselves negative thoughts and let our negative emotions take the wheel. This book transformed my inner monologue into my inner cheerleader. I've also found that it continues to hit me years after finishing it. I find myself accepting rather than fighting painful emotions and being kind to myself where I used to be cruel. (Vital to healthy self-esteem!)

Not Nice *by Dr. Aziz Gazipura[12]*

For me, an anxious, chronic people pleaser, Not Nice was honestly a revelation. Many, many anxious attachers also struggle with people pleasing.

10 Lindberg, I. (2018). The 21-Day Self-Love Challenge: Learn How to Love Yourself Unconditionally, Cultivate Self-Worth, Self-Compassion and Confidence (21-Day Challenges Book 6). Kemah, TX: Kemah Publishing.
11 Germer, C. (2009). The Mindful Path to Self-Compassion: Freeing Yourself from Destructive Thoughts and Emotions (1st ed.). New York: The Guilford Press.

12 Gazipura, A. (2017). Not Nice: Stop People Pleasing, Staying Silent, & Feeling Guilty...and Start Speaking Up, Saying No, Asking Boldly, and Unapologetically Being Yourself. The Center for Social Confidence.

If this is you, give this book the chance to change your mindset. Without a solid sense of self and the feeling that you have the right to be/feel how you want, there's no self to build self-esteem upon. This one is not a short read but if you struggle with people pleasing, bear with it. You'll come out of Not Nice feeling like a brand new person.

Your self-esteem is crucial to your happiness and your ability to let others love you. If you need to, this is a good place to slap a bookmark and focus on the work for a while. Therapy is absolutely not an overnight process. It can take years to start seeing progress. Your journaling is also something that will take time before you start recognizing changes in the way you think and feel. Everyday life can be busy. Even for the very motivated, I know the book recommendations at the end of these chapters can also take some serious time to knock out.

For me, I couldn't wait to change. I knew that the way I'd been living and loving was painful and I was ready to be a confident, self-loving, secure attacher *NOW*. Nothing was more frustrating than all the waiting while I did the work...except for the slip-ups, worries that change would never come, and feelings of hopelessness when confronted head-on with my issues despite all my hard work.

You'll get there. With time, persistence, and effort, you'll start to feel differently. Then you'll start to act differently. Little by little, things will change for you. But trust me when I say that it doesn't happen quickly. For the impatient like me, I recommend funneling that frustrated energy into doing the hard work. (And while you're at it, don't forget some leisure time, too!)

When you're frustrated, recognize that feeling and write it down in your journal! When you're feeling at your wit's end, book an appointment with your therapist! Obsessing over another bad date? Self-care night! There are so many tools and good things that you can replace that anxious and insecure energy with. This will be the focus of Chapter 3. We're going to dive into the tools and behaviors that will allow you to ditch the feelings of hopelessness and frustration and build your best life.

So whether you're bookmarking this and focusing on the work thus far or turning the page, I'm excited for you to read on.

"THE WAY TO GET STARTED IS TO QUIT TALKING AND BEGIN DOING."

- WALT DISNEY

CHAPTER THREE

CREATING YOUR BEST LIFE

What does your best life look like?

Maybe it looks like the images and clips clogging up your social media feeds. Your arms are spread wide, your back to the camera, and the background is filled to the brim with unreal mountainscapes. Or you're racing down a deserted freeway van-life style, independent and unencumbered by obligations, expectations, or to-do lists. Perhaps you're surrounded by luxury and fine things—a beautiful house, a fancy car, the newest electronics, and clean, modern lines. Or maybe your best life is the idea of a person, overjoyed to see you, gathering you up in an easy embrace, with love and affection to spare.

Whatever your paradise happens to be, what are you doing to get yourself closer to that?

The truth of the matter is, people who are living in a way that is true to what they really want are very easy to fall for. They live the kind of life that draws potential partners like moths to a flame. And even when they aren't partnered, they have a great time living their life. Fellow Anxious Heart, that could be you.

Are you feeling a bit deflated reading that paragraph? If you're like most people, the sad truth is that you may not be doing anything to get yourself closer to that life. If all you're doing is surviving your day-to-day life, managing to scrape by with the bills paid, food in your belly, and your job intact, you're at least in good company. Most folks are just maintaining the status quo. They're not falling behind, getting ahead, or daring to dream of anything beyond their daily routine.

They're stagnant. Are you?

This isn't the get-rich-quick chapter. I don't care if you ever make a million dollars. And unfortunately, I also can't promise you that following my advice will enable you to find that perfect love you've always fantasized about. But surprisingly (and don't shoot the messenger here), you can die without obtaining either of those things and still have lived a very fine life.

But how can I live a fine life without finding my "one true love"...!?

If you've hung your happiness on goals that can be wiped away by something as simple as bad luck, what leg do you have to stand on when those things disappear?

It's because a "fine life" isn't the destination. Think about it this way...

Let's say you work your tail off for years and years investing all of your free time and energy into that million dollar goal. One day, in your 60s, you realize that your account or assets finally add up to that magic number. What a feeling!

What an accomplishment! But how much of your life have you sacrificed to get there? How many evenings did you spend at work that could have been spent with friends and family building bonds and memories instead? In retrospect, was this a good life? Was it the kind of life you would have designed for yourself if you could do it over again?

Or imagine this: you finally meet your perfect mate! They're attractive! Witty! Passionate! And best of all, they also think that you're amazing. What luck! My god, you've waited so long for this moment. *Now,* surely, you can finally relax into the happiness that you always knew would come once you found a soulmate to complete your life. All of your miserable searching and waiting has finally paid off and bliss is yours for the taking...and then, for whatever reason (plane crash, you grow apart, infidelity, etc) fate takes them away from you.

The things that we dream about, those spectacular things that will make it so that we can "finally be happy," are often not real. Or rather, they're real, but they often aren't sustainable or realistic. And then, even if they *are* real, like a relationship or success or money... something as unexpected as a stock market (or plane!) crash can take that external source of happiness away in a moment. Not to mention, money or career goals can sometimes necessitate a life of *unhappiness* in order to achieve them!

If you've hung your happiness on goals that can be wiped away by something as simple as bad luck, what leg do you have to stand on when those things disappear?

Happiness researcher Sonja Lyubomirsky, in her book *The Myths of Happiness*, denounces concepts like new romance, home ownership, raises, and lofty goals as nothing more than temporary dopamine-boosts at best.[13] Boredom in our relationships and dissatisfaction with our partners can quickly make us question the role of romance in our long-term happiness. We may even find ourselves feeling lost and hopeless when we find that our relationships are not the happiness-generators that we hoped they would be. So what brings us real happiness?

Thankfully, Lyubormirsky makes sure to point us toward more certain paths to happiness. Building a life full of healthy platonic friendships and relationships is one. As anxious attachers, we have a nasty habit of idealizing a romantic partner as being the only person or thing which can bring us the kind of supreme happiness we dream of. It's not uncommon for an Anxious Heart in the beginning stages of love/infatuation to hold their beloved in higher regard than their career, hobbies, friends, family, even their own children (...!) sometimes long before they've gotten a chance to properly get to know the object of their affection.

Surely, the feelings that we get in the throes of romantic love can feel second to none. The euphoria! The pleasure! The intoxicating ups and downs… But these feelings are not happiness. At best, they are fleeting rushes of endorphins and dopamine that last only until the butterflies in our stomachs stop their fluttering. And even if one was to argue that feelings of passionate romantic love *are* happiness, they are certainly not sustainable. Where, then, should we place our happiness?

Let's start with one of the most obvious places: our relationships with others.

---

13 The myths of happiness: what should make you happy but doesn't, what shouldn't make you happy but does. Lyubomirsky - Penguin Books - 2014

Building Healthy Relationships with Others

Let's forget about romance for a second. How are your platonic and familial relationships?

First things first: do you have any? I'm talking about real, tried-and-true friends who you feel you could call in a bind who would have your back. These are the folks that you can tell your secrets to. They'll keep them, they won't judge you (too much, anyway!) and sometimes they've got some great advice for you, too.

I dated a guy who once said, "If my best friend called at 3am asking me to help him bury a body, I'd show up at his doorstep with a shovel and not ask any questions."

While this always made me laugh (and was hopefully a gross exaggeration!), it went a long way to describe the amazing bond they had. It's that "ride or die" kind of friendship that endures despite each other's faults and quirks. It was one of those friendships that felt more like family.

Do you have friends like this? Maybe it's your sibling or someone you've known since grade school. Maybe you don't even speak that often! That's okay. Just knowing that there's someone there if you *really* need them is an enormous comfort and can have a huge impact on your life and mental health.

Maybe you don't have any friends like this. This is where we take a good, hard look at your friendships. Our friendships say a lot about a person! After all, you've got to *be* a good friend in order to *have* one. And being a good friend is not simply asking how someone's day is or being super friendly whenever you see them at the gym. It's also not in the random favor here or there. Being a good friend is about genuine caring and commitment—resolving to have your friend's back when they're truly struggling and having that same level of care returned to you.

So often it happens that we anxious folks identify as givers, and it's the "getting back" part that trips us up. Is this you? Unfortunately, this kind of behavior can often net us less-than-genuine friends who are only in it for what they can get from us.

Many anxiously attached people I've talked to have the problem of give, give, giving until they feel drained and resentful and never feel like they get the same level of effort or care in return. Really, you don't have to be anxious to experience this, but no matter where you are on the attachment spectrum, if this is your experience then it's time for a lesson on what healthy friendship looks like.

Healthy friendships have all or most of these traits:

- You feel better after having interacted with your friend, not worse. Your friend gives you energy and positive feelings; it makes you feel good to be around them or talk to them.
- The friendship adds to your life; it does not detract or distract you from healthy things.
- Both people benefit from knowing one another. You will not find one person giving considerably more and the other taking more. Things feel like they are on even ground.
- Both friends are respectful and treat one another well.

- Both friends encourage each other's growth and are not threatened by change in one another. Similarly, they respect and honor differences in each other. A good friend accepts you for who you are and not who they want you to be.

- The friendship is not about power or taking advantage of or using anyone. Both friends are in it for the other person as much as themselves.

- Both friends are committed to the friendship; when one friend is upset about something, the other friend, being invested in the friendship, does what they can to patch things up.

- The friendship is not dependent on anyone doing anything for the other person. Each person is there, happily, of their own volition, simply because they enjoy the other.

Sure, just like in relationships, friendships have their ups and downs. There may also be some rather dysfunctional aspects of a friendship from time to time, without the overall relationship being "bad." But for the most part, healthy friendships just feel *good*. They're fun to be in. Having friends like this makes your life feel *better*.

If you're reading those bullets thinking *Yep. That's what my friends are like!* Nice work. You're probably already enjoying the positivity and happiness that your good friends bring to your life. This next paragraph is for the folks who are reading those bullets thinking, *No, my friends aren't like that at all.* Or, worse yet: *What friends?*

If you're someone without many friends, that may be one reason that romantic relationships haven't been working out for you. A romantic relationship can't survive under the weight of a person without other healthy connections to lean on. If you need your lover to also be your sole confidant, therapist, adventure buddy, downtime, and shoulder to cry on, that's simply too much to ask of a single person!

Romantic Partners Shouldn't Be Our "Everything"

A *lot* of people look immediately to their romantic relationship when they feel upset. You don't have to feel too guilty about this because it's basically written into our cultural narrative on romance: "Your perfect lover is going to be *your best friend* and once you meet them you will never have to face your problems alone ever again! They will always want to hang out, like all the same things you do, and be 100% ready and willing whenever you need a pick-me-up or feel the slightest bit bored."

The problem with this attitude is that it's unrealistic at best, and at worst…toxic. It's bad enough that we've been force-fed this narrative our entire life, but even if you *did* find someone who fit this description, it would be tragically unhealthy.

Our romantic partners were never meant to be our *everything*. In fact, no one can be that for us. And don't worry, this isn't the part where I tell you "only *you* can be your everything!" because I don't believe that's the right answer either. Humans are social creatures! This, reader, is why family and friendships are absolutely vital to our personal and relationship health.

Our friendships help ease the burden of life. We shouldn't have to shoulder all of life's trials alone. This task is made considerably easier with "a little help from our friends." Not a single person, but ideally a support system of lots of individuals with different skills to offer. We need this robust support system so that no one person is carrying too much for us! Every once in a while, our significant other can step into a helper role, but asking them to take on this position full-time (especially if they are the only one carrying that responsibility!) is asking too much of them.

We've got to quit drinking the Disney-happily-ever-after-Kool-Aid and wake up to how unhealthy it is to expect someone to fulfill all of our needs. How would you feel if your partner were unable to be happy without you? When would you have time to pursue your own interests, build your career, nurture your friendships, or simply be alone to unwind? You wouldn't! You'd be a prisoner, tasked with keeping your partner happy at all times. Now ask yourself; could this be what you've been expecting of *your* romantic partners? Have you been asking too much of them because you don't have other sources of happiness and support in your life? I know that I've abso-lutely been guilty of this many, *many* times in my past.

The truth is, it's not a romantic partner's job to satisfy all of our needs. It's our job to communicate what we need from a relationship and then decide if the way that they handle that information works for us. That's it!

Further benefits of having solid friendships in your life include:

- Improving your mood: Good times with friends can increase happiness.
- Helping you reach your goals: Friends encourage us to be the best versions of ourselves.
- Supporting us in tough times: It's vital to have someone to lean on in times of unexpected trouble or when we feel the burdens of life getting heavy.
- Boosting your self-esteem: The give and take of a healthy friend-ship makes someone feel valued and needed, raising feelings of self-worth.

Additionally, it really is rather hard to imagine a healthy romantic relationship occurring between two people who don't have a single good friend outside of it. Your friendships, *independent of your relationship*, are part of who you are. And one of the very key things about this part of us is that it will still be intact if/when our relationships fall apart.

Think about it this way: How free are you to be yourself, with all of your unique interests, needs, quirks, and flaws, if any of those things threatens your lover *AND* your only friendship?

If your lover is the only person you have in the world, you will be completely paralyzed by the fear of upsetting/losing them or driving them away, and will thus be unable to be your true self in their presence. How miserable is that!?

If you need any further convincing on this topic, Esther Perel has an eye-opening TED Talk entitled *The Secret to Desire in a Long Term Relationship*.[14] You can zip over to YouTube and give it a listen, or just let this summary soak in:

Passion is fueled by both partners maintaining an independence, separateness, or otherness. Our partners need to have some curiosity and mystery about us in order to want more. Togetherness, intimacy, and deeply knowing one another is wonderful; it breeds comfort and security and love. But passion? That fire can be stoked by nurturing a vibrant, fulfilling life in the hours/days away from your partner which will spark their imagination and curiosity.

14 (n.d.). TED. Retrieved October 4, 2021, from https://www.ted.com/talks/esther_perel_the_secret_to_desire_in_a_long_term_relationship?language=en.

Pick up your phone. Call or text that friend you've been neglecting. I promise that it will be good for you *and* your relationship.

Nurturing Your Friendships

So, what are some things you can do to make sure that your significant other isn't your only friend?

Introverts rejoice! You don't need a giant crowd. It only takes a few good friends for a life that feels fun, supported, and full. Knowing this, choose your friends wisely. They should be people you consider genuinely upstanding, solid folks, whom you feel good around. These friends should be people you can be yourself around. You'll also benefit from choosing friends whom you like and accept as they are, without glaring defects that make them impossible for you to be around.

Now, take this to heart because it is key: once you find these friends, *prioritize them*. This can be very tricky for us anxious folks, who unfortunately don't typically hold our friends as dear as our romantic prospects.

One of my worst anxious habits was leaving my schedule wide open just in case my partner *might* want to spend time with me. This left my friends feeling very second string and unimportant (and rightly so—that's exactly how I was treating them).

Now I make sure that I hold my friendships in high regard. I prioritize them, actively schedule time to spend with them regardless of what my partner is doing, and make sure that I check in on them every now and then.

Initially, I worried that prioritizing friendships would take away precious time with my significant other and damage my relationship. Instead, it actually did the opposite.

By prioritizing my friends, I was showing my significant other that I valued my time and my friendships. This made my significant other view my time and friendships as important, as well. I was also showing my friends with my actions that I valued them. It's not difficult to understand why a gesture like this would strengthen a friendship. Another important bonus to prioritizing friendships is that it gives our partners some space; this enables them to feel safer to come close to us.

Other ways that you can strengthen your existing friendships:

- Handwritten cards/notes: Holidays are made more special by handwritten messages from friends. You can also deepen friendships with personally written thank-yous for a thoughtful gift/ gesture, or a "Just Because" card expressing gratitude for their friendship.
- Be proactive in contacting them: Don't let yourself second guess this. *"They probably don't want to hear from me"* is typically just your anxiety and not reality. If you feel like chatting with someone, send them a message or give them a phone call. It doesn't have to be a long message or call, but don't let the months or years build up between contact.
- Be vulnerable: Don't be afraid to share deep thoughts with friends or lean on them when things start feeling heavy. The ability to be vulnerable with a friend shows them that you trust them with your emotions. That goes a very long way in deepening a friendship.

Reciprocity in Friendships

If you're overly anxious or have people pleasing tendencies, you may find yourself in lots of one-sided relationships and friendships. After all, in the dating world, it isn't difficult to find a people pleaser pining away in a lopsided "Situationship" or "Friends-with-Benefits" situation that they hope will turn into a legitimate romance. If this is something you struggle with, I feel for you because I've been there. With a tendency to be like this, we can find ourselves in unhealthy friendships, too!

Take a mental inventory of the quality of your friendships. If any of the following bullet points are missing (or you find that you're the only one offering these to the other person), you may want to reevaluate if this friendship is working for you:

- *Do they show a genuine interest in your life? Do they seem to listen to what you say, how you feel, and think?*
- *Do you feel accepted for who you are without judgment or pressure to change?*
- *Do they listen without invalidating your feelings or trying to change the subject back to themselves?*
- *Do they celebrate your successes?*
- *Do they do things that you enjoy as well?*
- *Do they engage you and invite you to hang out without your prodding?*
- *Can you tell them personal things and trust that they will not use that information to hurt you?*

With anxiety or low self-esteem, sometimes friends (even bad ones) feel like a lifeline. We find ourselves scrambling to keep them in our lives.

But it's important to ask yourself, *how does this friendship make me feel?* If you're spending lots of time with someone who criticizes you, competes with you, makes you feel anxious or exhausted, makes fun of you, or you find that your other relationships are suffering because of that person, you may be involved with them for the wrong reasons.

Sometimes we can rack our brains but still not know if a friendship is healthy or not. Try shifting your focus to what the friendship feels like. Do you feel drained by their presence? Are you walking on eggshells? Censoring yourself? Do you feel insecure, as if you have to be on guard around them? Are you hiding things from them about yourself?

People pleasers can even trick themselves into thinking that they feel *good* about a friendship that they're getting nothing out of. Feeling needed and important is often enough to hold our attention. But someone "needing you" is not enough for a healthy friendship. There should be just as much give as there is take on *both sides*.

Take a moment to evaluate your friendships. Write down some names. Think about how each person makes you feel as you write their name down. Is the overall feeling good, ambivalent, or bad/uncomfortable? What do you do for these friendships? What do they do for you?

We must hold on tight to our good friendships and make room for them in our lives, even when we have a shiny, new love interest. And if you're anxious, *especially* then. We must save our energy for the people who light us up and make our lives feel easier, better, and brighter.

Take Stock of Old Relationships

What if I told you that all of the things you just read that apply to healthy friendships also apply to healthy relationships? You might not be surprised, but have you ever looked at your romantic relationships through that lens?

Take away the attraction, the romance, the sex, the butterflies in your stomach, and review those bulleted lists. Have your past romantic partners also been good friends to you? Or were they one-sided friendships? This one might be hard to face. Many of my past relationships that I looked at in this new light did not hold up well.

Passion is fueled by both partners maintaining an independence, separateness, or otherness.

As anxious attachers, it would benefit us to start looking at romantic relationships in this new way. Most times, people end up spending a lot more time with their significant other than platonic friends, so it makes sense that this relationship should be one of, if not *the* healthiest one we involve ourselves in.

Think of how you acted in your most recent (or most serious) romantic relationship. Did you make room for your friends, hobbies, or passions? Did you abandon yourself or your interests in favor of spending time with your lover? Did you give up too much of yourself for someone who didn't treat you as a good friend would?

We *need* to change this pattern, Anxious Hearts. Love and romance should never come at the sacrifice of your identity, your relationship with your friends, or any of the things that you love in life.

A healthy relationship should *add* to your life, not take away from it.

Therein lies the problem for many people who have not built a full life for themselves for someone to add to. We sit around feeling miserable about all the ways we feel our lives are deficient, hoping that someone will come along and make us feel whole. Fortunately, the power to make your life whole rests entirely with you! Let's take a closer look at what you're working with.

Building a Healthy Relationship with Yourself

Having healthy self-esteem is the foundation for our ability to be in a good relationship with other people. Without genuine love and care for ourselves, we're unable to provide that to others, and instead we may spend our interactions with them trying to get those precious things that we cannot give ourselves.

Having good self-esteem isn't as easy as just "believing in yourself" or feeding yourself positive messages that you don't really believe. It comes from a constant, concerted effort to change your habits and the way that you treat yourself. The following are a number of self-esteem boosters that you can practice on a regular basis.

Establish Healthy Habits

We're all busy! And inside of our already busy lives, it can be tough doing things that are good for ourselves on a regular basis. To further complicate it, if you've already established *un*healthy habits, you've got the double challenge of unlearning some very ingrained behaviors and habits that may work against you in order to make room for the healthy ones. Start with the basics; commit to acts of personal hygiene daily that you may often skip or forget. Daily oral care (with flossing!), springing for a good face scrub that you resolve to use every night before bedtime, and a planned weekly bath (don't forget the candles!) can go a long way in sending a positive message to yourself about how you treat your body.

Schedule these things in and do them regularly until they become part of your natural routine. Once they become natural, you can add in new, tougher self-care habits; pick a regular morning walking route, commit to ten pushups per day for a month, commit to eight hours of sleep, or prepare healthy lunches for yourself every night before work. Whatever makes you feel like you're taking care of yourself is great.

Meditate Regularly

Make time to clear your mind or close your eyes and let your thoughts wander where they may. Finding a time to clear the noise in your head (or simply listening to what it has to tell you) can make a big difference. Learning to control or quiet our mind is like weightlifting; it gets easier with practice. If we're resistant to confronting or calming our thoughts, the unconscious processes in our mind will rule our world. We may even start to view our mind as the enemy! Making time to clear our thoughts or simply listen to them is a way to show ourselves love and respect.

Meditation and focus is a muscle! With practice, regular meditation can also help us resist the urge to ruminate on our anxieties or have our day derailed by intrusive thoughts.

Get Curious and Be Kind

You know that voice in your head that judges you for all of your emotions, reactions, feelings, and thoughts? Knock that off! Next time you hear that little voice berating you for something (anything!) try this instead: get curious. Ask yourself *why* you're judging yourself. What were the circumstances that brought the judgment about? Does it make sense why you feel the way you do? What could you do to avoid this in the future? Or, if it was inevitable, how could you go about accepting it? Kindness and gentleness here is important too. If a friend came to you with this same problem, would you belittle them for how they felt? Of course not! Be a good friend to yourself and be curious and kind when it comes to evaluating your own behavior and feelings.

Anxious attachers enjoy showing other people love. We're definitely less good at showing it to ourselves. By regularly treating ourselves kindly, we can redirect some of the love we show others back to ourselves. It's a vital step toward being able to accept love from others.

Discover Your Passions

Anxious attachers struggle with confronting their own desires, needs, and emotions. We're often so focused on others, that we don't even know what we, ourselves, like! In our journey to build a relationship with ourselves, we almost have to date ourselves. Put time and energy into discovering what it is that you love. Having a high passion for the things you love is something that makes you very attractive to potential dates. This can be a tough endeavor if you're not used to it, but stick with it. It *may* feel unnatural...until it doesn't!

Repairing the Holes

We've only got so much time. But perhaps even more finite than our time is the energy we've got to spend. You can have all the time in the world, but with no extra energy to pour into the things that are important to you, time is worthless. So let's think of your precious energy as gasoline in a giant tank. Now, let's find the holes. In which areas of your life are you leaking energy?

Your stressors create holes. The people who need more than they give back to you (often referred to online as "energy vampires") cause massive leaks in your tank. The blind spots in your life cause major energy leaks (bills that you don't pay on time, responsibilities that you avoid, etc.). You get the idea. Basically, anything that causes stress takes energy to deal with, which steals energy away from you that you could be using to build something great for yourself.

So do you try to fill your tank up when you're just hemorrhaging energy!? Of course not. First, you must repair the holes. Or at the very least, address them! Here are some more severe drains on your energy:

Working at a job that you hate or one that is very mentally taxing.
Needy family/friends who ask you to do things they could do themselves.
Ex-lovers or old friends whom you help simply to maintain the old connection.

115

Regularly engaging with people who drain you instead of energizing you.
Avoiding bills/repairs/health issues because they feel scary or overwhelming.
Mindless social media scrolling or binge-watching videos.
Wallowing in self-pity, making excuses, and/or giving in to your anger regularly.
Filling your body with highly processed, sugary, or convenience foods.
Avoiding regular exercise.
Loneliness resulting from neglecting your friendships.
Boredom eating/mindless snacking.
Refusing to set goals for the day/month/year.
Escaping your problems through excessive alcohol/drug/electronics use.

Sure, everyone has vices. And it's not a sin to indulge every now and then in the occasional sugary treat or awesome new TV show. And without a doubt, "all work and no play makes Jack a dull boy" and sucks much of the joy out of life. Additionally, not everyone can just quit their job or completely cut off family members/friends who are draining to them. But *balance* is the key here. All play/indulgence and little work leads to a life where nothing of great importance is created. And allowing unavoidable stressors to take over your life without addressing them or working to balance the bad with the good is also not a recipe for success.

A healthy relationship should add to your life. Not take away from it.

You've got to plug some of those holes so that you've got lots of extra energy to pursue the things that make your life great. Review that list again. Do any of those seem like things you do regularly? If so, circle them. And get your repair kit out, because they need to be addressed *now*.

If the list feels overwhelming, maybe just pick one bullet point and re-solve to find a way to make a big change to it. Even if it's just a minor repair, I promise that every single one of these problems leaks a massive amount of your energy that would be much better spent building good things in your life.

Have you decided on the thing (or things!) that you're planning on addressing? Good! I have found it helpful in the past to grab a sticky note (or a piece of paper and tape) and stick it on my bathroom mirror.

"This week, I resolve to address _____."

Perfection is not the goal here, but rather awareness of your engage-ment in that energy-sapping activity. We've got a lot of work ahead, and you're going to need all of your energy reserves. There are entire books dedicated to fixing problem areas in your life. So in the interest of keeping this book focused on attachment issues, I encourage you to take this one into your own hands.

Dedicate your next journal page to the problem areas in your life. It's easy to find them even without a handy bulleted list; just think about what is causing you worry or stress and write it down. Now, instead of trying to solve these, simply use the next week to take note of when they pop up. Notice where they pop up. And then once you have identified the when and where, brainstorm on ways you might go about addressing them directly.

If you find something popping up often (for example, unpaid bills), be proactive and use this opportunity to take a big step toward fixing it (e.g. buy a book on budgeting or automate your bill-paying). If it's a toxic friend-ship that causes daily anxiety, consider cutting down the time you spend interacting with that person. If it's physical discomfort centered around an unhealthy body image, find/create a simple daily fitness goal (5–10 pushups per day for a month). Anything that gets you in the routine of dealing with these stressors on a daily basis is going to put energy *back* into your tank. You're going to need all the energy you can get for the next part…

Learning to Love Your Own Company

Don't run, Anxious Hearts. This next section isn't for the faint of heart, but I promise you can do it.

One of the most disturbing things I learned during therapy was that anxious attachers often cannot stand to be alone.

The anxiously attached, running from time alone in our own heads, tend to leapfrog from relationship-to-relationship, seeking distractions and companionship like a lifeboat. Even outside of dating, well, it's hard to deny that we can be very clingy! Our friendships and connections are sacred to us and we hold them very, very close—sometimes too close. We're usually so busy getting good feelings from them (read: dopamine hits!) that we don't even realize that this treasured part of our lives can often be a big fat crutch.

No way. I just REALLY love being with my favorite people and there's nothing wrong with that.

Be careful with this justification. Your "extra strong love" may be more of a dependence than it is a healthy way to engage with the world. How do I know? For me, it was a simple challenge that my therapist suggested that opened my eyes to how unhealthy it was for me to constantly need people around.

"I challenge you to go on a trip alone."

Cue the record scratch sound.

I felt my heart leap into my throat. The very thought made my skin crawl. Can you even imagine why anyone would want to go on a trip all by themselves? The horror! The judging glances I'd surely receive from the part-nered folks around me! The boredom!? The loneliness!? Goodness, the list in my head went on and on...

No way. I remember saying to him. *No thanks. That sounds awful.*

So my therapist proposed a baby step of a challenge: "Go eat at a restaurant all alone."

This idea was also pretty terrifying, but doable. After all, I was looking forward to being able to have my favorite dish—a giant bowl of pho beef noodle soup—without having to convince anyone to go with me. Nervous, but with a determination to show my therapist that I could, I accepted his challenge.

Book in hand, I strode into my favorite local sushi joint. "How many?" the server asked immediately, his eyes searching for my lunch companion. "One," I said. I could feel the shame constricting my throat and embar-rassment coloring my cheeks. But him? He looked completely and utterly indifferent. He led me to the bar where I sat down and self-consciously pulled my book out and started reading. I hoped that the other restaurant patrons would just think I was waiting for a date to turn up. But a funny thing happened next. When I started to get into my book, the restaurant noises around me fell out of my awareness. The server interrupted to take my order, and before I knew it, I found myself totally engrossed in my reading, flipping the pages of my book while absentmindedly feeding myself delicious, hot noodles. When my soup was gone, I looked up from my book. I had been reading for over forty-five minutes. I enjoyed my meal immensely. And best of all, no one around me had even seemed to notice the girl eating alone at the bar.

Well. That wasn't so bad, I suppose.

I didn't have much to report to my therapist. I had completed his challenge without much fanfare and was ready for the next homework assignment. Really, I didn't even give it any further thought until the next time I was craving pho.

I had already begun scanning my phone for available friends I might invite when it hit me: I could just go alone. Why not? It went well the last time, right? Any feelings of embarrassment and solo-dining-shame had been fleeting at best and I was surprised to find that my memories of that meal were actually pretty…great.

I went back alone. The server recognized me and led me to the same seat at the bar. This time, he pointed at me as soon as I sat down and said, "Pho, right?" to which I simply nodded and quickly pulled out my book. This meal seemed to go even more smoothly than the last! I found myself really savoring my noodles, unhurried by any dining companion, and enjoying a leisurely reading pace, too.

I wouldn't have believed it if you'd told me back then, but today, solo dining is one of my favorite pastimes. I actually try to spend at least one meal every week or so out in public, totally alone. And crazier still—I look forward to these solo meals with the excitement of a child at Christmas. It has quite literally become one of my "happy places." The impact of this experience on me cannot be overstated.

I learned later in therapy that one of my biggest fears was simply being alone with my own thoughts. Does this idea bother you, too? The noises in my head were negative, critical voices that I'd attempt to drown out with company, distractions, and idle chit chat. My fear of spending time alone was really the fear of having to face the voice in my head without any distraction to soothe and distract me.

Are you also running from the voice in your head? Do you try to drown it out by distracting yourself with company? Are the words you tell yourself when you're alone too uncomfortable to be alone with? I know mine were.

Anxious attachment comes with a profound mistrust of ourselves. We don't feel confident in our ability to soothe ourselves when unpleasant emotions pop up. To cope, we find comforting distractions in other people. Even more unhealthy, we sometimes find someone who does the comforting for us (or someone who confirms those negative thoughts by echoing them). The experiment my therapist proposed helped me to build some trust in myself. I grew, solo meal after solo meal, to trust that my own company wasn't so bad. In fact, it could be downright pleasant! That single realization has led to freedoms I'd never known before.

I started planning evenings alone. Then I started enjoying evenings alone. Then, unexpectedly, when I found myself dateless for my cousin's out-of-state wedding, I decided to go *on my own*.

For me, that trip was a revelation.

To overcome anxious attachment, we must learn to rely on ourselves when things in our mind get uncomfortable. When the warning bells sound and we feel lonely, abandoned, rejected, disregarded, or cast aside, the very best thing that we can do to move ourselves toward hallowed secure attachment is learning to self-soothe. There are no shortcuts. We must learn to face our struggles more independently in spite of our discomfort.

Learning to self-soothe is, unfortunately, a matter of putting yourself in uncomfortable situations over and over again and slowly coming to trust that you can handle them on your own. It takes practice. It takes perseverance. It takes *guts*. For me, it also took probably hundreds of dollars worth of pho. But little by little, you'll start to feel it—confidence that when discomfort rears its ugly head, you have the power to stand up to it and stare it down until it passes. Learning to love your own company is a major step toward living your best life. Don't skip this one, reader. It may be my favorite new skill out of all the things I've learned thus far.

Underneath our Defenses

The question seems straightforward enough: what do you want? But is it really so straightforward and easy? Maybe not...

Have you taken the time to sit down and write out what it is exactly that you want out of all this? Out of what, you may ask? Well, out of love, of course. But also, out of life! Out of your very existence, even. Have you taken the time to pinpoint exactly what it is that sets your heart ablaze and causes it to light up?

Sadly, most people haven't.

It's a big job! It can also be an intimidating one. If you're like many Anxious Hearts who have never even let themselves have wants, where do you even begin!? I know that was my question the first time a writing prompt challenged me to figure out exactly what I hoped to get out of love and life. I felt a curious fog inside my mind when I tried to dig in and figure it out. Walls sprung up left and right. You may be feeling some of that now as I present the question to you.

There is a little trick I learned to get around those walls.

Sentence stems are a way to get quickly into your unconscious mind. They're an incredibly powerful tool that you can use to combat the over-thinking and defense mechanisms you've developed to avoid getting to the bottom of what you want. When someone asks us what we want, for example, our brains quickly jump into overdrive. We wonder what someone's agenda might be in asking us such a personal question. We wonder what answer they might be expecting from us. We wonder what we *should* say, or what the *right* answer is. We may even quickly spit out a lie, just to get that person off our back!

With sentence stems, we avoid this overthinking. We can quickly get to the bottom of what's really going on in our heads.

Finish the following prompts as soon as you read them. Don't over-think! Don't second guess! And best of all, there are no wrong answers. You may be surprised about what pops up for you. Ready to find out how you truly feel and what you want? Write your answers down if you've got a pen nearby! No pen? Try reading the prompts and simply finishing the sentence out loud. Pause between each question and really reflect on each answer.

I feel happiest when I…

It is very important to me that I…

I feel the most loved when…

I am really good at...

I feel respected when…

The thing I want most for myself is…

The thing I want most in a relationship is…

The thing I cannot live without in a relationship is...

Nice work. How'd that feel? If some of your answers surprised you, that's OK! Surprising answers have a lot to teach us about ourselves. This stuff may feel painful or shameful for you to look at. If that's the case, it's *vital* that you acknowledge these feelings sitting just beneath the surface of your awareness.

Okay, time for a change of tone. It's important to know what we want, but it's equally important that we get an idea of what kinds of things may be standing in the way of what we want. Take a deep breath, and answer these as soon as you read them, speaking your answers out loud or writing them down to reflect on later. Again, pause between each sentence.

I'm afraid I'll be rejected if I…

It feels like people push me away when I…

I cannot stand the feeling I get when…

I feel lonely when…

If I were stronger, I wouldn't allow…

If I were honest, I would admit that I don't like it when…

I feel disrespected/unloved when…

I feel rejected when…

In my experience, the answers to these questions pop up quicker in my mind but provoke a stronger response. Did you learn anything about yourself here?

It can be very hard to figure out what we want. I know that my own mind tends to rebel the second I ask questions like this. I can feel the walls coming up, objections flying, and a voice that tells me that I should focus on others and not myself. It's all well and good to be concerned with the people around you, but if you've got no idea what you want, you're in danger of losing yourself in other people's wants.

Self-abandonment, the idea that our wants/needs aren't important, is a hallmark of anxious attachment and also a killer of intimacy.

One trick I use to get around my walls is to ask, *"if anything were possible, and nothing was standing in the way (money, family, friends, work, obligations, etc.), how would I want this to look?"* The answer is very often fantastical and impractical, but it reveals a lot. Try to boil down the underlying message in your wildest dream. Ignore the millions of dollars raining from the sky; are you taking someone you love on a lavish vacation? Disregard the beautiful beach house; does your fantasy have you spending lots of uninterrupted time with someone special to you? Your dream scenario may have you looking hot after months of personal training and elaborate gym routines; but at the root, is the purpose of all that training to gain the attention and/or admiration of your lover? Look for the basic desires underneath your fantasies to realize what you value and want most.

Chasing what you really want, and investing your energy into moving toward those things, is the only way to get to your best life. Are you making time and energy deposits daily into a situation that looks different from what you hope for? If so, you're actively creating a life that you don't want. In order to build that best life, we need to put all of our energy into building something that matters to us.

Anxious Hearts, make yourself a list. On that list, include just a handful of things that are very, very important to you about how you relate to someone romantically. These should be things that you want for yourself that make your life better. On my list are things like, "I want to feel respected," and "In a relationship, I want to feel like part of a team." It's not easy to stay true to this list. Even now, years into practicing this, I still struggle regularly. But without this list, I wouldn't have the focus I do now. To find our way out of relationships and situations we don't want, we need to know what we *do want*.

You may tell yourself that you're fine just exploring your options for now and can't be bothered to pinpoint your wants. That's not all bad! After all, you can't know what you want if you've never experienced anything (or anyone) before. I'm not saying that you should cut off everyone who doesn't check off every single box you have in mind for the perfect partner. Anyway, the perfect partner doesn't exist; every person you meet will have flaws and quirks that you're not so crazy about.

The trick is to pay attention to how things feel. Let that be the guide for what you want. When you find things about others that make you feel good, take note of it! When you find traits or behaviors that make you feel bad, pay attention there, too. It's up to *you and only you* to decide what feels good and bad in your relationships, and to determine what you want. When you figure out what you want don't take your eyes off of it.

126

Even more important for Anxious Hearts: don't let anyone tell you that you shouldn't want that thing.

I hope that this chapter impressed upon you the importance of finding love in places other than a romantic partner. In her book, The Strength in our Scars, Bianca Sparacino writes about finding love in every aspect of our lives. In my favorite poetic paragraph, she specifically mentions finding love and meaning in "the smell of our favorite places," and also "whenever we hear our favorite songs," or in "growth, change, messiness, and the beauty of [messing] up, and making mistakes..."

This sentiment should inspire any anxious attacher with hope. Too often we hear that romantic love is the be-all end-all of happiness. Sparacino, myself, and countless other authors and researchers disagree. When we can learn to find the beauty, joy, and happiness in even the most mundane things in our lives, we will truly be living our best life, no matter what our circumstances or relationship status. It's possible, Anxious Heart, if we can only redirect our focus. There's a lot of light that we miss in the world when we are laser-focused on obtaining love. Especially when our focus is to obtain it "at all costs", with no regard for our true desires and needs.

My hope for you, reader, is that you can learn to draw some love from places other than romantic relationships. Yourself, your friendships, your family, your passions, and the world around you...these are rife with love if you can pull your gaze away from romance long enough to notice. Truly, this sentiment probably won't dampen your search for love. But my hope is that it can help you understand the importance of honoring what we want and need within a relationship and the idea that we can find a lot of the love we seek outside of a romantic partnership, too.

Homework/Reading Assignments

You can't get anywhere if you don't know where you want to go. Spend time with others. If you're able to, spend more time dating and determining what traits you enjoy and which ones don't work for you. Now, if you haven't already, it's time to make a list of the things that you want for yourself.

- *Make a list of what you want in a relationship.*

You can draw from previous experiences or start noticing now on your dating journey what feels good and what doesn't. However you decide, now is the time to think hard about those experiences and start separating them out into "must haves" and "deal breakers."

Make these lists in your journal so you can refer back to them whenever you meet someone new, or if you feel like you've lost sight of the things you want. Remember to add a date to your entry!

My therapist had a great challenge for me back when I was dating and feeling quite conflicted about how to decide if someone would be good for me or not. I was looking for a very particular set of qualities and feeling frustrated that no one I went out with lined up with them. My boxes were too specific! It's no wonder now, looking back, that the tall, brown-eyed, intellectual, nerdy-but-also-athletic, emotionally intelligent, jet-setting, affectionate-but-stoic man-of-my-dreams never showed up…what a list to fulfill!?

My therapist suggested this: when you're dating, make a list of what you don't want. This list should be easy to write because it will ideally only contain things that would be absolute no-gos. He suggested some things like "disrespectful," "unaffectionate," "unmotivated," etc. I wrote down qualities that I knew either would make me miserable or would be incompatible with how I wanted to live my life.

Now, if I discovered that someone who wanted to date me had any of those no-go qualities, I would immediately but politely bow out. But if they were clear of these deal-breakers, my therapist suggested I just keep myself open to the unique things that they had to offer.

What an eye-opening experiment! I met so many interesting people when I took this advice, and I also learned a lot about what I was looking for (and what I didn't want). So in the spirit of this:

- *Make a list of what you don't want.*

Even if you're very clear on what you do want, it's a good idea to keep the traits you don't want in mind so that you can stand firm when you see deal breaker traits pop up. It's hard to stand up for what we want when we're face-to-face having a lovely conversation with an attractive potential partner. It's even tougher to be firm about what we don't want when we're already emotionally attached to someone...so don't wait too long to bow out if a deal-breaker is present.

Remember, it's never too late to decide what you do or don't want for yourself. You're allowed to change your mind even if you've already had poor boundaries or allowed behavior you don't like in the past. This is your life and your story! It's up to you to create the kind of life that others want to be part of, and you enjoy living. Now, some reading to reinforce these ideas.

Suggested reading for this point in your journey

If you're still with me at this point, hopefully you've already discovered quite a bit about yourself. We're going to keep that momentum going by picking up some intense books. You're ready for it!

Codependent No More *by Melody Beattie*[15]

When a friend recommended this book to me, I didn't even know what "codependent" meant. Regardless, they were so adamant that I read it, that I simply took their word on it. I am so glad I did. Codependency isn't just a concept for the struggling partners of alcoholics. This book is for anyone who consistently puts themselves second. It is for anyone who is disconnected from themselves and the things they want.

Codependent No More Workbook *by Melody Beattie*[16]

If your codependency reading is striking a chord, you might also consider picking up Melody Beattie's companion workbook to help you really get to the bottom of codependent behavior and also figure out what you want and need.

He's Scared, She's Scared *by Steven Carter & Julia Sokol*[17]

This book has a lot to say about women (and men!) who pursue commitment-averse people. If you're an anxious attacher, you're no stranger to trying to get closer to people who are perpetually pulling away from you. I never in a million years fancied myself as a commitment phobic. In fact, if

---

15 Beattie, M. (1986). Codependent No More: How To Stop Controlling Others and Start Caring for Yourself (1st ed.). Center City: MN: Hazelden.
16 Beattie, Melody, and Melody Beattie. Codependent No More: Workbook. Hazelden, 2011. .

17 Carter, S., & Sokol, J. (2012). He's Scared, She's Scared. New York: Bantam Books.

asked, I would have confidently identified as just the opposite. Surprisingly, this book opened my eyes to my *own* contribution to the lack of commitment in my life.

Your life is going to get a boost from the increased focus you put on making it great. If you're working hard with the information you've gleaned thus far, hopefully you'll start feeling your friendships and relationships begin to improve. The people around you may begin to notice too! Bolstered by improved relationships and a renewed focus on the things that you want for yourself, you're in a great position to begin doing the work.

What work, you ask? This is where we really dig in and get to the root of your problems. We'll aim to get to the heart of why you act the way you do, strive to understand yourself and your behavior in earnest, and finally, take steps toward changing your mindset so that you can be free of anxious or destructive thoughts, feelings, and actions.

This work is best done with the help of a trusted, knowledgeable therapist. If you haven't found one yet, I recommend doing that now if you're able to. As an anxious attacher, there is much work to be done. But with the foundation of an improved, happier life and more energy to draw from, it's time to start digging into your biggest problems.

Are you ready? Let's go.

"OPPORTUNITIES ARE USUALLY DISGUISED AS HARD WORK, SO MOST PEOPLE DON'T RECONGIZE THEM."

ANN LANDERS, ADVICE COLUMNIST

CHAPTER FOUR

BECOMING SECURE

Have you ever taken a deep dive into your mind? Do you have any idea why you think/do the things that you do? Well, you're in luck either way. That's exactly what this chapter is about. For now, we're going to shift away from looking at the people in our life and investigate a little closer to home.

Does that confounding brain in your head sometimes feel like it's working against you? I know mine does from time to time. But if your love life isn't working, you should be. This is where the real work comes in.

One good thing about being an Anxious Heart is that we *know* we have work to do. (This is in contrast to the avoidant attachment style who may be more inclined to think that the problem rests with their anxious partner.) A hallmark of anxious attachment is low self-esteem, and while challenging to live with, this state means that we easily accept that we've got areas to improve on. So pack up your pity party and let's get to digging.

Identifying Your Patterns

Hopefully, the pages of the journal you bought back in Chapter 1 are filling up. If they're still mostly blank, don't fret. Journaling can be *tough*. It can be especially tough if you're not crazy about writing. I have known many journal-keepers who prefer making lists to writing long paragraphs of texts. Some draw. Others have pages filled with stream-of-consciousness style writing that doesn't make much sense but can be a fantastic emotional outlet. I created The Anxious Hearts Journal with prompts specifically for Anxious Hearts to help make the writing process easier. However you get your thoughts down on paper, you're doing great. Slowing down and writing our thoughts out can help us organize and really acknowledge what we think, how we feel, and what we want. Consistency is key; just keep doing whatever works for you.

For the next journal entry, take a moment to think about what kinds of unhealthy patterns have been holding you back. You may feel some resistance when you ask yourself this. It can be hard to identify our unhealthy patterns and admit how we get in our own way. Give yourself grace!

If you need some prompts, the following questions can be helpful:

- What do I notice myself doing in relationships that causes me trouble?
- What seems to work well for other people that I can't quite figure out?
- What patterns do I notice in my relationship history that I wish would stop repeating?

Pay close attention to how you answer these questions.

If you find yourself resistant to writing these down and answering them, then it's even more important that you do it. If you're worried that you won't be able to articulate the right thing, put that worry to bed and just start writing. If you feel like you have no negative patterns and your dating life has just been a big jumbled mess, that's okay, too; simply write down what you notice is not working for you. You don't have to use this entry to solve your problems. Acknowledgment is the goal.

Now that you have them written down, take some quiet, uninterrupted time to think so that you can really analyze your answers. What you should focus on is *how your romantic relationships look and what they have in common that*

> **Without intentionality and being conscious of why we do what we do, we are doomed to stay stuck in our harmful patterns.**

doesn't work for you. Maybe you're someone who exclusively dates people who are physically distant. These would be long-distance partners or those who spend most of the relationship physically absent from it. Or maybe you have a tendency toward the emotionally unavailable—married, tortured, stoic, or those with wandering eyes? We're looking for patterns that you don't like. They may be tough to find or glaringly obvious. They will probably also be tough to face.

But one thing is for sure, you can't heal them if you can't see them. So let's bring your recurring relationship snafus out into the light.

Breaking the Patterns

Without intentionality and being conscious of why we do what we do, we are doomed to stay stuck in our harmful patterns. Breaking free of them can be the hardest part of healing.

You might even clearly see the ways that you're screwing things up for yourself. The destructive patterns that you seem to repeat in relationship after relationship might keep popping up no matter how different you think each new partner and scenario are. Even when you resolve to act differently, you might find yourself playing the same old role, feeling frustrated and not sure why you end up in the same situation every time. Is this your struggle?

No matter what your attachment style, people tend to get into relationships in a very haphazard way. We stumble or fall into them. We let our heart, instead of our minds, take the reins and we fall into the old traps of chasing "attraction" or "sparks" or "potential."

When we pursue love without intentionality our unhealed trauma often leads the way. Anxious Heart, don't beat yourself up for this. It's more common than you think, so at least you're in good company. But I'm here to tell you that in order to find relationship happiness, you *must* change your patterns. Or at the very least, become more aware of them.

You may feel resistance upon hearing this. I know I did. As soon as I was confronted with the idea that I had to do whatever it took to change my behavior patterns, I felt my mind throwing up excuses—reasons why it was too difficult, impossible, or brainstorming other, easier ways to get to happiness. Even though I badly wanted change, the path to get there just seemed too tough.

Even if you're reading this and thinking, *"Yes! I'm ready! Let's do this!"* you may not appreciate how tough it really can be to change the way that we relate to people and develop romantic feelings, a process that—thus far—has been largely automatic and unconscious in our lives.

Changing our patterns can be painfully slow and arduous; but it *is* possible. So let's be smart about this.

If your goal was to run a marathon or lift 200 pounds or lose 50 pounds, you wouldn't attempt these things right off the bat and expect success, right? You'd start small. Baby steps, even! First you might run around your block every morning until you felt like you could go a little farther. You might get a small, manageable dumbbell and start lifting small sets every day until that routine becomes too easy. You might replace your lunch every other day with a salad or sign up for a fitness program. The relational changes that you need to make in order to better your life aren't so different from this. It would be counterproductive (and perhaps even a bit harmful to your health) to dive right in headfirst and expect success in changing your attachment behavior and patterns right away.

Drastic changes to your life (such as initiating a divorce or breakup, or practicing jarring behavioral changes on the people you love) can be as destructive as running a marathon without training, crash dieting, or trying to lift more weight than you can handle. Please don't put this kind of pressure on yourself. Don't expect to finish this book (or any other, for that matter) and be cured of your relationship and behavioral problems. That's simply not how this stuff works.

If there's a big change that you want to make in your life you can find success through *setting goals of increasing difficulty and consistently practicing what it takes to achieve them.* This is great news and should make the burden of change feel a lot less scary.

You don't need to force yourself to be drastically different than you are right now. You simply need to learn new ways of engaging and focus on practicing them in small ways every day. Continue to do this until those tasks become easy and then you can add new, tougher tasks into your routine.

Here are some small changes that you can implement as an anxious attacher that will help you move slowly and steadily toward secure attachment.

Speaking Up About What You Want

Anxious Hearts can be die-hard people pleasers. We effortlessly set aside our own wants and needs for those of the people around us. Thanks to this impulse, we often find ourselves muzzled when the time comes to speak up about what we ourselves want and need. In the beginning of my journey, the simple question of *"what do you want?"* could induce a full-on panic response in me. This one may not be so tough for you, or you might be like me and find yourself breaking into a sweat when it comes time to make your wants and needs known. So what can a people pleaser do to break the pattern?

Practice making small declarations and see how they feel.

"Actually, I'm not a fan of that restaurant. Is there anywhere else we might go?"
"I'm feeling tired. What do you think about staying in this evening?"
"This music isn't really my style. Do you have something mellower?"

Later on, I'll recommend a workbook that helped me immensely with this. If confrontation makes you nervous or you're just plain bad at asserting yourself, an assertiveness workbook can be a valuable tool in helping you make the baby steps that it takes to get to the big leagues.

"I'm having a really bad day. Could I have a hug?"
"I think it would be fun if we took a vacation together. What do you think?"
Or even the dreaded…

"We've been hanging out for a while and I really enjoy your company. What are your thoughts on making this official?"

Okay, I know. Let's not get too far ahead of ourselves…! (But wouldn't that be something?)

If you are already in an established relationship, you may be finding it terrifying to speak up about what you want. I know that it felt that way for me. Our work as anxious attachers is to practice speaking up about the things that we need constantly, pushing through the fear and discomfort, until it becomes easier and more natural. If you find that your partner doesn't support your learning to speak up and is, instead, continuously shutting you down, you may consider couples counseling. Their resistance to you voicing your needs doesn't mean that your needs are wrong. It's okay to need things, Anxious Heart. Rather than excessive needs, this is more likely an issue of poor boundaries on both of your parts.

Setting Boundaries

Boundaries are key to any healthy relationship. They also happen to be something that we Anxious Hearts can be really, really, tragically bad at. Whether you're a chronic boundary-crosser or suck at setting your own, this part is for you.

Boundaries may be such a foreign concept to you that you're not even sure what they are! You may have trouble recognizing others' boundaries and how you may have been violating them in the past.

A great metaphor for boundaries is to think of them like the fencing around your house. Your house is you, and your boundaries are the fencing around it. When we let people disregard our wants/needs, we are allowing them to climb over our fence and trample our yard. They may stomp the flower beds or drive up onto the lawn. You can feel this unpleasant intrusion in your body when your wants/needs are disregarded. This can feel like discomfort, a building resentment, stress, anxiety, guilt, and fear.

Ways that people cross and disrespect our boundaries can be almost unlimited. It can happen when they try to change your "no" into a "yes," when they borrow something and don't return it (or return it in disrepair); they may invade your personal space, disrespect you verbally, show a lack of respect for your time, or guilt you into doing something that you don't really want to do. And many times, we allow the boundary crossing without any consequence.

That's when the feelings of resentment, anxiety, and despair really start to pile up. Our discomfort around the boundary violations may come out in strange or unexpected ways. It comes out in our passive aggressive comments, our lack of effort, our feelings of powerlessness; you may find unexplained health issues popping up—gut trouble, aches and pains, or insomnia.

Medicine may ease the symptoms of our boundary violation wounds, but they will not cure them. These maladies can only be healed by learning to set healthy boundaries for yourself and with others.

Additionally, setting boundaries is a step that can only be completed after you determine what your boundaries are. Decide what's important to you and practice not letting people disregard that. Some baby steps for boundary setting may sound like this:

"You know, I don't like it when you call me at the last minute with your plans. If you want to hang out, I need at least a couple hours' heads-up."

"I'm feeling nervous; can we come back to this discussion in an hour after I collect my thoughts?"

"Sunday is my day to unwind. I'd love to hang out on Monday, though."

Practice saying "no" without further explanation. You don't need to defend any of the reasons why you do or do not want to do something.

There are scores of fantastic books on boundaries. A great one is Boundary Boss by the wonderful Terri Cole.[18] Her content and online courses have done more for my ability to set healthy boundaries than any other source I've found.

And if the idea of speaking up for yourself inspires terror, remember that every time you do, you are communicating to yourself and others that you are brave, full of self-respect, and that your needs matter. For sure, this shift can actually change the way that others treat you.

Practicing Independence

I touched on this one in the last chapter. Our fear of spending time alone is a huge barrier to our independence. Baby steps in this area can

---

18 Cole, T. (2021). Boundary Boss: The Essential Guide to Talk True, Be Seen, and (Finally) Live Free. Louisville, CO: Sounds True.

include scheduling alone time or embarking on solo activities. They don't have to be big! But regular, independent time and activity can be an amazing confidence builder and help us to feel more comfortable when we're alone and rely less on others; something Anxious Hearts tend to do far too much of.

Another way to boost independence is self-soothing. You can practice resisting the urge to overshare or spill your guts to a significant other or friend and instead settle into your journal, visit a trusted therapist, or indulge in a lengthy meditation session. Identify crutches and cut them out. Resist calming your nerves in unhealthy ways and learn to sit quietly with your thoughts (uncomfortable as they may be!)

Independence doesn't mean cutting out everyone and everything that we rely on. Rather, it's boosting our ability to take care of ourselves. It's an area that Anxious Hearts often struggle with, and a skill that *all* attachment styles find very attractive.

Assertiveness is Sexy!

I can remember feeling full of words. Words about things I wanted and needed. Words about thoughts that I had. Affectionate words that I felt bubbling up inside me that I held down for fear that they wouldn't be received well. Words to defend myself or share my hidden parts, and words that were silly for no reason at all. And I remember stuffing them all down out of fear.

I worried that others would judge me, say "no," or pull away. I worried about the pain of rejection and kept myself small because I was sure that it was a safe alternative to being denied, shut down, or criticized. Does this sound familiar?

142

Anxious Hearts, we are a nervous, worrying sort. Sometimes it seems like there is no limit to the disaster scenarios we can dream up. *What if they say no? What if they think I'm dumb? What if they don't care that my feelings are hurt? What if they reject me for expressing this? What if they tell everyone and I die of embarrassment and lose all of my friends and then the economy crashes and civilization devolves into roving bands of anarchists and I'm left all alone, and, and…*

Whoa! Breathe, my friend.

Even without the roving anarchists, hearing a simple "no" can be quite scary or can *really* hurt.

Asserting our wants and needs can be terrifying. But with practice, it can also be incredibly empowering. And with mastery, it can be a fantastic tool for building healthy relationships. (Not to mention, it's also super sexy!)

As Anxious Hearts, we often daydream about being direct, confident, superheroes who can say exactly what we want to say when we want to say it and not fear a negative response. We can even find ourselves drawn to people who seem almost omnipotent in their ability to assert their wants/needs and enforce strong boundaries (hello, avoidant attachers!). But we can hone this skill in ourselves, too.

First, try some baby steps. Jump on opportunities to make little assertions and congratulate yourself when you do. Tell the people close to you that you're working on being more assertive and would appreciate their help—I found that my friends and family in particular were more than happy to find opportunities to encourage me to speak my mind.

The workbook at the end of this chapter made a huge difference for me. It immediately shuts down the idea that assertiveness and boundaries are "encouragement to steamroll people" or "something that will push away the people I love" and sets readers straight about what they really are: a healthy way to express the things that are important to us.

If you need any further convincing, think about how you feel when other people express a need. No matter your attachment style, it's likely that you care about what other people want and need. Is it really so far-fetched to imagine that other people also care about what you want?

Being able to express what you want and need serves a few very important purposes:

- You earn respect from people.
- People learn to trust you to be honest about what you want.
- You build intimacy with someone by letting them see the real you.

All of these concepts are explored deeper in the workbook at the end of the chapter. Don't let this one intimidate you, Anxious Hearts. This kind of work can help you find your long-buried voice.

Sitting with Discomfort

Carl Jung, the father of analytical psychology, said, "All mental illness is an inability to withstand discomfort."

Think about any of the things that bother us. We aren't actually running from those things, but rather, we run from the feelings that those things create within us. We live in a pretty comfy world, really. Nothing is trying to eat us. Food is just a grocery store or drive-through away, and modern medicine can cure most of our everyday ailments. So what is an anxious brain to focus on?

That's right: good old-fashioned discomfort. It makes sense. We come kicking and screaming into this modern world wired with these very old, very primitive brains that are trained to be constantly on the lookout for danger. In our comfortable houses filled with food and friends and comfort, there are no lions to be dodged, no dangerous buffalo to hunt, no clan leaders to appease, essentially, nothing life-threatening at all.

So what do we do with all of the alarms in our head that are constantly on high alert, scanning for signs that our life is in danger? Unfortunately, we redirect their attention toward the modern things that we worry about.

Relationship conflicts, minor fender-benders, your new iPhone taking a swim, bad drivers, fights with our family members—all of these things can inspire the kind of fear, anger, and anxiety that once kept us alive. Granted, relationship unrest in our cave days was cause for alarm; a major rift within our ancient family groups could mean we were booted from our clans, thereby losing our protection, food supply, and social support. However, most of the things that we focus our anxiety on nowadays aren't as big a deal as we make them out to be.

However, simply knowing that these things won't kill us is not nearly enough to keep our panic at bay. Thankfully, there is comfort to be found in the practice of learning to sit with discomfort.

Cognitive behavioral therapy, a method of treatment in counseling that promotes an awareness of our thoughts, feelings, and behaviors, encourages learning to identify our fears and discomfort, rather than blindly reacting to them. Often, our biggest problems come from our attempts to escape discomfort. Alcohol, nicotine, drugs, phone addiction, and other unhealthy coping mechanisms are among the many negative ways that we try to distance ourselves from feelings we don't like. For the anxiously attached, our protest behavior is one way we run from the discomfort of handling our tough emotions.

What's the process of an anxious attacher employing a protest behavior?

Well, I'm so glad you asked!

- First, we perceive our love interest or partner as pulling away.
- Second, our alarm system goes off—the big one. This is the same system that's meant to alert us when we lose our connection with our caretaker—the kind of thing that would be potentially fatal for an infant or child, but is notably less life-threatening to an adult in a romantic relationship.
- Next, we experience the extreme discomfort that the alarm system is meant to provoke. We may feel anxious, nervous, afraid, pained, suffocated, or the like. If these feelings seem big and very hard to ignore, that's because they were designed to be!
- Lastly, we resort to whatever method we've developed for reestablishing that connection and making the alarm system (and thus, our discomfort) quiet down. Unfortunately, Anxious Hearts, this often means unhealthy protest behavior like excessive contact attempts, provoking jealousy, or any number of unhealthy behaviors we commonly resort to.

Contrary to what we're trying to accomplish, these kinds of behaviors don't bring our partners closer to us; rather, they work to push our partners away.

What if we had a higher tolerance for discomfort? Or even better, effective tools for quieting the alarm system without resorting to harmful protest behavior?

Let me ask you something unexpected: how long can you hold your breath? (Don't worry, I'm going somewhere with this!)

It's not something that I'd really thought much about since I was a kid at the public pool. But recently, as an adult, I was challenged to find out. I found the experience to be extremely uncomfortable. Forcing myself to keep my lungs filled when they were positively screaming for air, feeling the involuntary contractions in my chest as my body attempted to get some oxygen without me, and watching the numbers tick by on the clock wondering how much more I could stand. It felt like torture.

But I tried it. And I even managed to surprise myself; I ended up holding my breath for a solid 45 seconds longer than I thought I could. And with a little practice, I found myself able to do it for longer and longer.

The experience reminded me of the zen reading I'd done that promoted *leaning into and accepting discomfort* rather than trying desperately to escape it. If you can withstand discomfort, it doesn't have as much power over you. It also means that discomfort won't define your ability to be happy or hold you back as much.

The more I practiced holding my breath, the less intimidating it became with each session. I knew with certainty that I was not in danger when I started feeling the urge to gasp for air. I found myself less fearful of the discomfort of my lungs reaching their limits. And with time and practice, the lungs' capacity expands. This, too, is how it is with our ability to withstand uncomfortable feelings, sensations, or thoughts. If we immediately run, no tolerance can build up. We remain trapped in our fear, not knowing if we are safe or how much we can withstand. We will find ourselves hiding behind our defense mechanisms, never able to face the things we don't want to feel/think. But if we lean into the discomfort a bit, training ourselves to be calm in the face of rising discomfort, we will be able to handle greater unpleasantness with increasing grace and strength.

So I ask again, in regard to discomfort rising within you: how long can you hold your breath? Do you immediately run? Or do you aspire to stand up and face the things that you don't like to feel?

As an important caveat, this metaphor does not apply to abusive relationships. If you are with someone who is causing you mental or physical abuse it would be foolish to try to teach yourself to withstand more abuse. The same thing applies in a relationship where you feel positively starved for something (validation, affection, understanding, etc.). This would be akin to asking someone to practice holding their breath without ever coming up for air.

But in a relationship where positivity also exists and it is temporary or *occasional* discomfort which is plaguing us, we can greatly benefit from knowing how to keep our cool when things feel uncomfortable. The ability to remain calm in the face of discomfort can allow us to hold onto ourselves and breathe through temporary pain. That way, we can calmly collect ourselves and feel empowered to say what we need to say later when we are feeling more balanced.

Truth be told, it's scary to say the things that we want to say! We worry about rejection, looking foolish, not being able to get our needs met, or worse, that our partner will abandon us for speaking up. When we can get more comfortable with the discomfort that arises from speaking our mind, we are freer to speak our minds. When we are freer to speak our minds, we are more able to create a relationship that deeply honors our wants, needs, and boundaries.

Additionally, the ability to withstand discomfort empowers us to *respond* rather than react. Keeping our cool, rather than responding with a stress response, allows us to choose how we respond to a situation instead of more typical (and often regrettable) knee-jerk reactions. This can be difficult to learn, for sure. But with consistent practice, it is a relationship game changer.

Why We Might Overlook a Secure Attacher

If you've been on many dates, Anxious Heart, there's a great chance that some of your dates were secures. *Not possible!* You protest. *I would have recognized such a rare, sparkling gem!*

I hate to be the bearer of bad news, but secures often slip through our radar undetected because we tend to find them downright boring. In a cruel, confounding twist, an Anxious Heart will often find themselves on first date after first date, sitting across the table from folks who are kind, pleasant,

well-read, intelligent, and otherwise good-on-paper, but just don't seem
to get our hearts pumping. (It should go without saying that this is a very
important pattern to become aware of.)

So what is it about the safe choices that feel so…boring? My best friend
suggested, "Maybe your 'picker' is broken?" He wasn't wrong. In fact, I now
believe that he was spot on.

The research is clear on why insecure attachers (anxious, avoidant, and
disorganized alike!) can't seem to drum up the interest for those unfortunate
"safe" choices and find themselves in volatile/toxic/roller coaster relationships over and over again.

Put simply, an activated attachment system (the warning bells) feels
like love to us. Without the warning bells going off in our heads ("He's too
distant! She's too clingy! They seem like the type that will leave me!"), everything is just calm, quiet, and yep, you guessed it—boring.

*So are you telling me that I should force myself to feel attracted to my boring
dates!? That sounds awful. I am definitely not going to do that.*

Of course you aren't, Anxious Heart. And rest assured that I'd never
ask you to settle for someone who doesn't make your heart thump. I am a
romantic and the idea of settling for someone whose conversation puts you
to sleep would go against every romantic and artistic impulse in my brain—
and likely yours, too. But there are a few tricks I have up my sleeve to retrain
your brain in order to help fix your broken "picker."

- **Recognize that the warning bells of an activated attachment system
do not equal love.**

The prime reason for our broken "picker" is the fact that the highs and lows of an activated attachment system feel like love for the insecurely attached. The turbulence is familiar—it is likely how you felt as a young child attaching to your parental figures, or when you were forming early romantic attachments. Because of this, it is what you identify with "love." When the red light is flashing "DANGER!" throughout your brain because Mr./Ms. Wonderful isn't texting you back, the feeling that it is vital that you get in touch with them to reconnect and win them over feels like passionate interest.

That "gotta have them" feeling you get when pursuing someone who is difficult to pin down is what we foolishly use to gauge how valuable they are to us. Our warning bells are ringing loudly and we say to ourselves, "Wow! I must really like this person. Is this love?"

The highs and lows of an activated attachment system feel like love for the insecurely attached.

Reader, let me be very clear: *this is not love.*

The feeling that you absolutely must be with them, that you must reconnect or win them over at all costs, that the alarms in your head are going crazy and you must silence them by obtaining proof or reassurance of their love…

That feeling is not love, and additionally, it's a positively horrible reason to pursue someone.

There are other words for this feeling! Infatuation. Limerence. Puppy love. Whatever you want to call it, it can feel both phenomenal and painful and many people chase this feeling exclusively. It's the stuff romantic movies and songs are made of. But it's still not real love, and definitely not a good reason to lose your head chasing it.

- *Learn more about why/how your attachment system becomes activated so that you can heed the warning for what it is (and what it isn't).*

There are many, many books dedicated to attachment theory and how it works and the many ways that it influences our relationships. And while there are no true shortcuts, hopefully the following will both sound familiar and serve as an explanation that you can refer back to when you start hearing those warning bells on a date—no psychology degree needed.

Remember the "Strange Situation" experiment from Chapter 1? Psychologists believe that our attachment systems were wired when we were infants (or changed/affected during formative sexual/bonding experiences) to sound off during certain upsetting conditions (namely, the threat of abandonment or rejection).

For secure attachers, they bonded with caring, responsive, reliable attachment figures. Because of this, they associate the good feelings (familiarity, safety, attachment, and thus love) with someone who makes them feel calm and secure (just like their original attachment figure).

For us insecure attachers, the story is very different. Our early attachment figures were perhaps distant, inconsistent, critical, unreliable, or otherwise not attuned to our needs. Our warning bells rang constantly in our heads around (or when we thought about) our attachment figures. For this reason, we learned to associate anxiety and worry with love. It also taught us that love and attention is something that we need to earn through good behavior; something that we must remain hyper-vigilant about lest it be taken away. From that young age, an activated attachment system began to feel like "home" for us. And without knowing why, we grew to seek out those alarms when selecting romantic partners.

We don't want to use our activated attachment system as a radar for love. When we can realize that it is feeding us a false positive, we can become more able to avoid troublesome romantic situations for ourselves.

* ***Practice heeding your attachment alarms for what they are— red flags.***

This is much easier said than done, but, with practice, it can be done. The easiest way to shift your perspective about your raging attachment system is to shift the language you use when you feel it firing up.

I know that many times in the past I would sit across from a date, bored to tears by their interest, availability, and mutual effort, and say to myself, "This person is boring. I must not be interested." Without the feeling of an activated attachment system, I falsely assumed that I could never come to love that person. We must stop using the words "exciting/boring" to gauge the "rightness" of a potential partner. This is what has been leading us astray. Pick better words to look for! Is your date "intellectual," "kind," "interesting," or "attentive?'"

Additionally, slow your roll, Anxious Heart! It takes more than a single date to really get to know someone. Too often, we're guilty of diving in at the first intense feelings we sense toward someone. This will take some practice, but holding back our commitment/fantasizing gives us time to assess whether or not someone really would be a good match for us, or whether we'd be strapping in for another roller coaster ride. The "spark" that we typically run toward is not a good indicator of compatibility at all.

Some great questions to ask yourself during this slow, multi-date assessment phase would be:

Do they respond to my texts/calls in a manner and timeline that makes me feel valued?

Do they react to my expressions of interest with equal interest or delight?

Are they open and respectful about relationship needs and boundaries?

Are they reliable and consistent?

Do they make decisions with me (as opposed to for/in spite of me)?

Do they compromise well?

Do they seem comfortable with commitment after a reasonable amount of time?

Do they introduce me to their inner world (friends/family/personal interests)?

Do they express feelings of affection for me?

Now, no one is perfect. Everyone has issues and many great partners are not going to get an A+ in all of these areas. But understand that missing any of these bullet points are going to make a relationship with them more complicated. And only you can decide if the struggles you encounter when trying to date someone are worth your effort.

- ***Find a secure couple that you can spend some time around, and pay close attention to the behaviors/words between them that you want in your own life.***

Thankfully, it's relatively easy for us to identify and admire healthy relationship dynamics in other people. Take advantage of this and grab yourself a role model couple and pay attention to the things they do and say within their relationship that you think you'd like in your own relationship.

Does your role model couple seem very comfortable expressing affection for one another? Add that to the list of things you want for yourself! Do they seem especially respectful and considerate of each others' feelings? Write that down! Maybe you notice that they're very good at diffusing fights when things start to get heated? Being that disagreements are part of any healthy relationship, that would be another excellent relationship behavior to aspire to.

For us insecure attachers, it can be super tough to sit ourselves down and decide what we want in a healthy relationship. Having healthy role models also helps give us perspective so that we can see that the push-pull relationship roller coaster that we're used to isn't what we want.

So you can see now why it's important to give extra time and consideration to a potential partner who feels more safe/boring than exciting, right? We've likely been chasing "exciting" for a long time! How's that been working out for us? If you don't address it, that broken "picker" of yours is going to continue leading you into tumultuous relationships. But with awareness, understanding, and intentionality, we can overcome our need to chase that dangerous spark.

To recap, here's the list of what you can do to retrain your picker:

- Recognize that the "warning bells" feeling does not equal love.
- Learn about why/how your attachment system becomes activated.
- Practice heeding an activated system as a red flag.
- Find a role model couple and pay attention to their relationship.

155

These are some great, very powerful ways that you can begin to heal and steer yourself toward secure attachment and better dating choices.

Get in Your Head

Even without a partner, there are some surprising ways that you can learn to become more secure in your relationships. Visualization is one powerful tool to add to your repertoire.

Did you know that your brain has a hard time telling the difference between what you experience and what you imagine? Obviously, this doesn't mean that you can't discern between real life and fantasy. But when it comes to learning, the brain sometimes can't! Consider how imagining anxiety-inducing scenarios in detail makes you feel. A plane crash, a snake about to strike, a painful shot at the doctor's office. Can you feel your heart rate rising? When you think of a disaster scenario within your relationship, your body may feel instantly anxious, depressed, or otherwise uncomfortable even though you're just imagining it. Thankfully, this principle can work to your benefit, too! When you imagine wonderful, comforting things happening within your relationship, your brain may get a dopamine boost—you feel good even though nothing has happened!

These good or bad feelings brought on by your imagination can create and strengthen pathways in your brain. Have you ever heard the phrase "neurons that fire together, wire together"? When you make a habit out of imagining yourself acting in healthy ways within your relationship, it can help hardwire your brain to help you become this way. This can be especially helpful for people who have trouble with intimacy.

For many people, things such as prolonged eye contact, hand-holding, and giving/receiving compliments is extremely uncomfortable, despite wanting very much for these things to be part of our relationships. When practicing them is not an option (for example, when you are single) or too uncomfortable to be able to do regularly, we can make a point to visualize ourselves engaging in these healthy behaviors.

An imaging study led by University of Colorado Boulder and Icahn School of Medicine showed that imagination and visualization can be a powerful tool for anxiety-related disorders and overcoming them. Practicing a fear-inducing behavior in our mind can serve to slowly train our brains to be unafraid. They found that real and imagined exposure to threats were not that different at the whole brain level. Imagining the threat but without negative consequences actually worked to reduce fear.[19]

How powerful is that? Imagining our fears *without negative consequences* can actually reduce our fears. Do not take this tip lightly. Visualization is an extremely powerful, low risk, and easy way to address some of our biggest fears.

Destructive Communication

One of the hardest things about being an insecure attacher is the feeling that relationships are not places where we can get what we need. In my own life, relationships have always felt hard. It was as if I was always trying, or fantasizing about the way I wanted it to be and constantly finding myself in relationships that never matched up with my desires. This was no accident. In retrospect, I was almost completely unable to voice my desires out of fear that my partners would leave me. One of the biggest barriers to making a relationship fulfilling for us is a lack of good communication.

---

19 Cumella Reddan, M., Dessart Wager, T., & Schiller, D. (2018). "Attenuating neural threat expression with imagination." Neuron, 100(4), 994. DOI: 10.1016/j.neuron.2018.10.047.

For some people, it's not for a lack of trying! But unfortunately, there are no partial points to be awarded for communication that doesn't quite hit the mark. Frustratingly, bad communication can be worse than none at all and sometimes set us back in our attempts to get what we need. We may think that we're communicating our needs to a significant other when, in reality, we are pushing them further away. Some examples of bad communication include but are not limited to:

- Sarcasm
- Hinting
- Sending mixed signals
- Being indirect
- Game-playing
- Withholding information
- Being critical/insulting
- Lying/white lies
- Communicating while emotionally activated

Even at small levels, these communication faux pas can be incredibly destructive in intimate relationships.

The Gottman Institute, a marriage research institute that has studied couples for over 40 years, has written extensively on what they believe are the four most destructive communications between couples. They've dubbed these "The Four Horsemen." They are:

Criticism
Defensiveness
Stonewalling
Contempt

In his 1992 study, Dr. Gottman was able to predict which couples in his study would eventually divorce with a 93.6% accuracy based on the presence and frequency of these four behaviors between the couple.[20]

While you may think of yourself as someone who communicates well and works hard to express your needs, it is important to look closely at the things we say to make sure that they aren't laced with any of these four deadly elements. Here are some surprising ways that The Four Horsemen show up in our communication as anxious attachers:

Criticism

Being critical of our partner's behaviors/words

Never believing our partners are "getting it right"

Believing that our partners aren't working hard enough to show us love/affection

Defensiveness

Refusing to acknowledge our part of conflict or our partner's needs

Feeling that we are incredible partners and not part of the problem

Stonewalling

Withholding our wants/needs from our partners

Withdrawing from them when we feel abandoned/neglected

Contempt

Comparing our partner's behavior unfavorably with our own

Feeling superior—like we are an amazing, loving partner and they are not

20 Buehlman, K. T., Gottman, J. M., & Katz, L. F. (1992). How a couple views their past predicts their future: Predicting divorce from an oral history interview. Journal of Family Psychology, 5(3-4), 295–318. https://doi.org/10.1037/0893-3200.5.3-4.295

So how can we turn our destructive communication habits around and start communicating in ways that make our relationships safe, satisfying places to be for both ourselves and our partners to be?

- ***Be Direct***

Anxious attachers especially are prone to indirectness. Often this is out of a fear of rejection, or a lack of knowledge about how to communicate healthily. Whatever the reason, indirect communication is often the culprit behind painful misunderstandings and/or toxic relationship environments.

Sarcasm, the withholding of information, and passive aggressiveness are also types of indirect communication—saying what you need without actually saying it. Try to avoid these at all costs when it comes to the expression of your needs.

- ***Talk to Your Partner, Not Everyone Else***

When it's scary to confront our partners about the things we aren't getting, it becomes very tempting to talk to everyone else about it. Anxious Hearts, you *must* stop this behavior.

It may feel good to vent to your friends and family about the many ways that your relationship or partner is hurting/bothering you. And there are times, no doubt, when a good long chat with a trusted friend can help us see our problems and the solutions more clearly. But one very damaging thing that anxious attachers tend toward is an inability to confront partners directly with relationship issues. This, paired with our tendency toward over-reliance on other people, can spell disaster in a relationship.

(As an interesting aside, avoidants struggle with an over-reliance on themselves to solve relationship problems, cutting their partners cleanly out of the problem-solving process. Truly, when partners cut each other out of the conflict and problem-solving process, intimacy suffers and no one wins.)

Although it can be scary—terrifying even—practicing the skill of communicating directly with our partners about relationship issues is a way to build trust, intimacy, and problem-solving power within our relationship. Honing this skill can also create an atmosphere of mutual satisfaction.

- ***Don't Be Afraid to Ask for What You Want***

What would your life look like if you weren't afraid to ask for the things you want? More specifically, what would your relationship look like? The possibilities of this thought can be staggering to an insecure attacher who has never experienced it before. But this isn't a fairy tale. It's possible. In fact, it's more than possible; with practice, it's very doable!

When you learn to identify your patterns, break the harmful ones, be assertive, sit with/through discomfort, and manifest the kind of relationship that you dream of through intentional choices and positive habits, you'll find that your voice gets louder and clearer all the time. Right now, it may be terrifying to ask for your needs. *What if they say no? What if they reject me?* If someone runs away when you state your needs, that's the universe carrying away what isn't good for you. Don't follow.

When what we want becomes clear and we learn how to express it without any insecurity, things start to change. *Big* things. Our power within our relationship begins to grow. We stop feeling so disempowered and start feeling like our relationship is a safe place, a place where needs are met and mutuality thrives.

When you allow your needs to be buried underneath your partner's, you lose yourself in a relationship. Slowly, you find your partner's respect and admiration for you being chipped away. The tendency is to morph into someone who can meet all of their needs and expectations, but this isn't what we aspire to in our relationships. Anxious Hearts, we want more. We deserve more. It's vital that we learn to ask for more. Our relationships will never be safe, satisfying places for us until we do.

And to close out this chapter, I want to touch on a sensitive subject that many partnered anxious attachers ask me about all the time. *What do I do when I am in a relationship with someone who refuses to do any work on themselves or the relationship?* Let me be the first to say, I know how incredibly painful this can be. I know what you're thinking: *if they cared about me, they would try harder.* Anxious Heart, I can promise you that your partner's reluctance/refusal has much more to do with their own struggles and nothing to do with your worthiness. In this situation, you have two paths. The first path is to work on yourself and see if your self-work changes the atmosphere of your relationship. Your emerging security might inspire your partner to come closer and do their own work! In the event that it doesn't, the other path becomes the best solution: decide that you need a partner who can support you and your shared relationship, find a support system in friends, family, or a trusted therapist, and make your escape. Whatever you decide, trust that you're doing the best you can for yourself, and give yourself and your partner grace.

Homework/Reading Assignments

Whew! You made it!

That chapter may be the toughest one of the entire book. Learning self-compassion/emotional regulation, assertiveness, breaking our difficult patterns, and healthier communication with our loved ones is huge. These things truly are the paving stones on the path to healthy relationships and learning them is genuinely hard work. It can be especially tough if they are new concepts to us.

So with that said, I want to congratulate you for making it this far! You are doing amazing things for yourself just by being here reading this. You should take a moment and give yourself some mental kudos or an honest-to-goodness pat on the back.

Now here are your homework assignments!

Read **The Assertiveness Workbook** *by Randy J. Paterson.*[21]

Wait a minute, why isn't this in the "Suggested Reading" section? Because, reader, for the anxiously attached, assertiveness training is that important. I am assigning this book to you as a homework assignment and not just suggested reading. The reason being, anxious attachers are notoriously conflict-avoidant, passive, and lack the ability to assertively address problems directly to the people we love.

---

21 Paterson, R. (2000). The Assertiveness Workbook (A New Harbinger Self-Help Workbook) (1st ed.). Oakland, CA: New Harbinger Publications.

Do you remember the term "protest behavior" from way back in Chapter 1? It was describing our unhealthy attempts to express unhappiness or unmet needs. This unhealthy behavior is killing our relationships. With assertiveness training, we can learn how to directly express our needs to our partners in a way that commands both attention and respect. This eliminates the need for protest behavior. The benefit is multi-layered: we get to act in a way that makes our partners respect us more, we develop trust in (and a respect for) ourselves when we take charge of making our needs known, and we also grow intimacy within our relationship by letting our partners into our inner world of needs and desires.

Learning to be assertive (as opposed to passive, passive aggressive, or aggressive) with our needs is one of the surest paths to secure attachment. So, you can see why I'm so adamant about you developing this skill now, can't you?

Suggested reading for this point in your journey

It's not enough to simply know ourselves and what we want; we still have to communicate with and relate to others well in order to have healthy relationships. And to have great relationships, we have to get serious about our communication skills. Level up your communication and your self-care with the following books.

Difficult Conversations: How to Discuss What Matters Most
by Douglas Stone, Bruce Patton, and Sheila Heen[22]
It's one thing to know how to express love and affection for your partner. It's another thing entirely to be skilled in bringing up difficult or

---

22 Stone, D., Patton, B., & Heen, S. (2010). Difficult Conversations: How To Discuss What Matters Most (1st ed.) Illustrated edition. London: Penguin Books.

uncomfortable things with them. It's also, unfortunately, necessary for both people's happiness. This book will teach you that conflict is not the verbal wrestling match you think it is. When approached with curiosity and treated as a learning experience, conflict can actually be an incredible opportunity for increased intimacy.

The Miracle Morning: The Not-So-Obvious Secret Guaranteed to Transform Your Life (Before 8AM) *by Hal Elrod[23]*

The Miracle Morning aims to transform your morning into one that includes a life-changing routine. Every day, your first hour will include several tasks of your choosing, including but not limited to, exercise, meditation, positive affirmations, journaling, and other positive, life-boosting gems. Use this book as a springboard to establishing those healthy new habits. After all, that's part of doing the hard work! A feeling of power and purpose in our life can go a long way in establishing our independence and self-worth.

Hopefully, by this point, you've had some big moments, changes in perspective, or are slowly noticing positive changes in the ways that you interact and connect.

You may even be itching to wade back into the dating pool with all of these new skills and attitudes under your belt.

So if you're ready (and only if you're ready), let's talk about getting back out there and establishing healthy love.

---

23 Elrod, H. (2012). The Miracle Morning: The Not-So-Obvious Secret Guaranteed to Transform Your Life (Before 8AM). London: John Murray Publishing.

"BUT WHAT IF I FALL? OH, BUT MY DARLING, WHAT IF YOU FLY?"

ERIN HANSON, POET

CHAPTER FIVE

ESTABLISHING HEALTHY LOVE

OK. You're doing the work. You're focusing on building up your friendships, your interests, and your self-esteem. You think you may finally be ready to date again. Maybe you've even downloaded that dating app you keep deleting. You swore you wouldn't be back, but here you are again, swiping away. Except this time, you have some tools in your belt.

So why is this still so terrifying?

Dating as an anxious attacher is something else. And honestly, no matter how secure you become, you're probably going to always have anxious tendencies. Attachment style, while not permanent or static, is still fairly hardwired. If you're an anxious attacher and feeling stressed, your default is to seek connection in a big way. In times of high stress (hello, like when you're *online dating*, perhaps?) don't be surprised if you find yourself falling back into unhealthy habits and behaviors. Don't beat yourself up for this! Notice what you're doing, take time to come back to a calmer state, and gently correct the behavior. (Also, don't forget to be gentle with yourself as this stuff takes time and practice!)

Obsessing, chasing, craving closeness and intimacy (often with those who have not earned your trust yet), experiencing difficulty trusting, oversharing on a first date, or worrying that a date will abandon you before you even know their last name…! Rest assured, Anxious Heart, you're not alone in having these worrisome thoughts. But take comfort in the fact that you're also not doomed.

Remember from Chapter 1 that roughly 20% of the population suffers from anxious attachment and we feel your pain. That includes me! I have been one hot-mess of a date, girlfriend, and spouse and no matter how secure I become through hard work, practice, and awareness of my issues, I still find myself freezing up or fawning over the object of my affection when the chips are down.

So what do you do when you feel yourself acting anxious?

- Stop. Notice what you're doing.
- Don't beat yourself up for having this response.
- Let yourself return to a calmer state.
- And gently correct the behavior.

Just because anxious tendencies persist, it doesn't make your journey pointless! Awareness is everything. And thankfully, catching yourself early enough in troublesome behavior can stop a problematic situation *before* it gets out of hand. So hit the pause button on that dating app. Stop the swiping and daydreaming for a moment. Seriously, delete it if you have to. I promise we'll come back to it later. You're going to want to get this chapter under your belt before you start chatting up those eligible singles.

This last chapter is all about how to jump back into the dating pool without any fear of drowning. There's a lot that you can do to protect your heart without shutting it down. And if you're currently in love or partnered or married, stick with me. There's a lot you can learn here that can help you in your current relationship, too! (I'll give you permission right now to skip over future sections that don't seem relevant.)

We'll explore how to tell if you're ready to date, how to deal with extreme feelings while casually dating, green flags, red flags, and how to recognize and accept healthy affection and attention. Whether you're itching to get out on that next first date, or the idea of meeting someone new still strikes fear into your heart, grab your journal and get comfortable, Anxious Heart. We've got work to do!

Dating as an Anxious Attacher

How does dating usually look for the anxiously attached? We anxious types will meet someone interesting or hop on an app feeling plucky and swipe away to our heart's content. You might mingle out in the real world with single folks and project an air of confidence and cool. You're having a good enough time. You may be in your pajamas with a glass of wine while you peruse Tinder, or idly swipe on Bumble while Netflix drones on in the background. Maybe you field Hinge messages while you cook? Flirt on multiple different dating apps with strangers? Or perhaps you swipe right while sitting on the toilet!? At this point you're not stressing about this *at all*. You feel cool and desirable. Worthy. Maybe even...*cocky*.

Maybe you even hit it off when messaging a person or two? You might be feeling excited, cautiously optimistic, dropping a mention of the dates to your friends or family, even. Because dating is easy at this point, right?

Before any hopes, dreams, or expectations (that is to say, before any attachment), we anxious folks can be cool as a cucumber. We may even brag about how independent and choosy we are as we callously reject potential dates that we deem not good-looking enough, too nerdy, too shallow, or surprisingly too *needy*.

Look at me! You think. *I'm doing great! I'm not anxious at all!*

Bolstered by this newfound confidence, you start to settle in. You let yourself start to dream. You let yourself start to really like someone. But as soon as you do, familiar feelings start to materialize...

As soon as you realize that this person could be a viable candidate, BAM! All of your cool immediately flies out the window. Do not pass go, do not collect $200, proceed immediately to a jail cell of nerves that you have created for yourself. Because you know that the moment you believe they could be someone special, the solution to all your loneliness, the answer to your lack of worthiness...you're *sunk*.

From this point on, nothing is easy. None of your other dating candidates hold a candle to this person. You daydream, you might snoop on them online, you might even start obsessing. Worry is soon replaced with anxiety. The cool, detached person your date initially met crumbles away to reveal a clingy, nail-biting, overthinking doormat.

Every encounter is replayed in your mind for clues. Thoughts race. *Do they like me? What did that look mean? What can I do to impress them? When they asked about next weekend, was that an invitation, or were they just curious?*

170

When can I see them again? Do they even want to see me again?
Am I foolish to think I have a chance?

Or maybe you're able to maintain *some* of your cool. But you know the moment any intense feelings enter the picture, you're in trouble. You find yourself hopelessly dangling from a string, at the mercy of whomever it is that gives you butterflies.

Even if this is how it has always been for you, it doesn't have to be this way. Let's chat about how to date like a secure attacher.

Some Tips and Tricks

It probably doesn't surprise you at all to hear that dating is *a lot* easier and more fun for the securely attached. Don't get me wrong, hardly anyone really enjoys the process. But it's not nearly as excruciating when you don't have to contend with the rise and fall of your very self-worth depending on how the date goes.

There are things that you can do as an anxious attacher to make dating easier on yourself. These can be very counterintuitive to the popular dating advice you may have grown up with or read online, but bear with me. The dating advice you're used to isn't geared toward calming an activated attachment system or healthily communicating with potential partners. At best, the advice you're used to advocates inauthentic game-playing and manipulation. But we can do better than that. We're shooting for honesty, true confidence, and the kind of behavior that attracts healthy, compatible partners to us.

These dating tips are specifically geared to help make things easier for you, the anxious attacher who would like to partner up with someone who can accept you, love you, and be excited about the unique things that you bring to the table.

Before the First Date

Before you ever set up a date with anyone, be on the lookout for signs of attachment styles. There are plenty of clues everywhere if you know what you're looking for. These can be gleaned from real life interactions if you're scouting for dates in the real world, from online dating profiles, or from chat interactions before a first date.

- Do they talk comfortably and without hostility about themselves and others, feelings, intimacy, and past relationships? Do they seem free and relaxed? If it's easy to be in their company and conversation flows openly between the two of you, chances are good they are (or lean toward being) **secure**. This is exactly the type of date you're looking for! This may be someone who doesn't hold grudges against an ex-partner, has great self-esteem, doesn't shy away from sharing about themselves, and shows a genuine, healthy interest in you too.

- A fellow anxious attacher can be a bit trickier to spot. Anxious attachers can often be quite charming and open; they can also be laser-focused on making people like them and building a quick, intimate connection. This can often look like confidence and openness, but be sharp! Do they sound like they are never, or hardly-ever single? Do they overshare emotions, intimate details, or ask very prying questions a little bit too early?

These can be signs of an **anxious attacher**. If you're discussing a date with another anxious attacher, be prepared for the sneaking suspicion that for some reason, you're just not interested.

- As someone with anxious tendencies, you need to be aware of whether or not you're sitting across from an **avoidant attacher**. Warning signs would be someone who is unwilling to talk about their feelings and instead focuses on career, hobbies, and other topics that aren't too personal or deep. Beware of a lack of serious relationships in their past or a noticeable disdain for (or idealization of) past lovers. Someone who comes on very strong and then seems to pull away without warning should also set off alarms for you.

It's important to note here that attachment style alone is not a reason to write someone off. We can find happiness with *any* kind of attacher who is aware of their issues or is communicative and willing to work on their problematic behavior and ideas. But we should be aware that when we are wading into the dating pool, each attachment style is going to present its own special mix of challenges for you. It's up to you to decide how much you can handle and how much challenge you're willing to take on to be in a relationship with someone.

I had a friend compare these choices to different modes in a video game. In your dating life, do you want to play on easy mode or hard mode? Dating another insecure attacher is absolutely possible, but quite a bit tougher than dating someone secure.

While Casually Dating

If you're an anxious attacher (or lean that way), you probably have a tendency to get tunnel vision for the first person who tickles your fancy.

Stop doing that.

It may sound counterintuitive to every fiber in your being, but you absolutely, positively must date around and/or get to know someone relatively well before you make the decision to ignore the rest and focus on one person.

I know in my own experience, the moment I developed more than a passing interest in someone, everyone else on the dating field faded away. But this kind of focus often blinded me to the incompatibilities and harsh realities of my love interest. Without having anyone to compare them to, I hoisted my date firmly up onto a pedestal, ignored red flags with determined, willful ignorance, and kept them firmly on that pedestal until the relationship crumbled.

One method anxious attachers may employ is to *see several people at once* so that you are able to weigh them against one another and figure out what you like and need.

This technique may sound cruel, but with good boundaries, it can be an amazing tool in your belt. My rule was that I would not get physical with anyone I was casually dating (beyond a simple end-of-the-night peck) unless I had decided to see them exclusively. I would also be open about the fact that I was casually dating others (but not physically involved with anyone). I found that my dates were very accepting of this, and seemed reassured by my openness about it.

174

What you're looking for in this process is a stand-out candidate, not a reason to excuse an individual's bad behavior.

By seeing multiple people at once, your anxious attachment doesn't get the opportunity to latch on to any particular one. Sure, you may be rooting for one above everyone else! That's natural and expected. But by keeping your options open, you're letting your dates speak for themselves and compete against each other for who can best fulfill your needs. This way, you can vet them based on who is bringing you the most positive feelings. This is *much* easier to determine when you're not working from a scarcity mindset.

Perhaps Date #1 texts very regularly, giving you a comforting sense of investment and security. Date #2 loves to spend lots of quality time together engaging in recreational activities that you both enjoy. And Date #3, despite being smoking hot, can't seem to find time during the week to text or call.

Keeping the other two firmly in the game, guess which anxious attacher is **NOT** going to be daydreaming about Date #3's dreamy eyes while simultaneously worrying about why they didn't call? That would be you, my friend. You'll be too busy laughing at the meme that Date #1 sent you this morning, or wakeboarding with Date #2.

Seeing multiple people casually gives us the opportunity to be ourselves and get out of our heads. The key is to keep your options wide open until one clear candidate proves their trustability and compatibility. That way you don't become hung up and find yourself excusing bad behavior from a single candidate with only one or two good qualities.

This is also the perfect time to start opening up about your needs and relationship expectations. Start the conversation about what you'd like a relationship to look like early on. Rather than making it a laundry list of demands, make it a discussion! Ask your dates what kinds of dating/relationship needs *they* have and what a relationship means to them; this is vital if you want to know early on if you'll be compatible!

And also, compatibility aside, the concept of *workability* is also very important. Disney movies have led us to believe that when we meet our fated soulmate, all the pieces will fall into place and everything will be magically easy and blissful. I hope you're sitting down for this truth bomb; that simply doesn't exist. *All* healthy relationships require good communication, openness, and compromise and hardly anyone you meet (let alone someone you're attracted to who is also attracted to you!) is going to be rocking the exact same needs as you.

Workability is the idea that you can listen to someone's needs and wants and say, "I can find a way to comfortably work with that." From there, you both develop a game plan that includes effort, compromise, and enthusiasm that allows both people to feel like they are winning.

When Things Start Getting More Serious

So what happens when it's time to make your selection?

Maybe on your wakeboarding adventure, you discover that Date #2 is rocking some serious abs. You also find that this person is positive, open, and makes you feel comfortable talking about anything that comes up. You decide that you'd like to see where things go with them (and hopefully see more of those abs…am I right?). After a kind, but straightforward goodbye to Date #1 and #3, you march bravely down the path to impending couplehood with Date #2. Now that things are feeling a little more serious, it's time to get *very real* about your needs.

This isn't the time to panic or be timid. You're probably starting to really like this person and are worrying about scaring them away. Don't be afraid of this. Counter to every anxious thought in your head, this is actually a good thing.

Wait, what!? I don't want to talk about what I need if it's going to scare someone away…

We're looking for someone who won't shy away from a partner who has needs. We're looking for people who celebrate us having needs, who encourage us to state these needs, and communicate with us about needs in a healthy, open way. We're looking for people who will *feel good* to be in a relationship with—no eggshells needed!

Your goal here is to be *so* real about your needs that the people who can't handle them will naturally fall away. It may be tough to let them go but trust that you're doing yourself a huge favor. We're throwing the small fish back. We're weeding out the tourists. We're saving our trust and affection for someone who says, "I'm so glad you told me that." Not, "I think you need too much."

> **We're looking for people who celebrate us having needs…**

If you can determine that someone won't work for you *before* you get attached, you'll be in a much better position to let them go. So during this early phase of dating, before you become attached, be sure of your needs. Define them, write them down, stand by them, and make them known. And most importantly, be fully prepared to walk away if those needs of yours don't work for your potential love interest.

You will not be "scaring away the love of your life," as I've heard many an anxious dater lament. After all, can you really imagine yourself finding long-term happiness with someone who doesn't want you to need anything?

As anxious attachers, we tend to idealize our partners and potential candidates for partnership. In the throes of passion, we imagine that they are the only ones we could ever feel so strongly about. This can blind us to big incompatibilities and prevent us from standing up for what we need in a relationship. Before we have a chance to idealize, we have to let people be exactly who they are and allow them to run away from us if that's what they want to do. And what is even tougher to accept is that we have to let them go without chasing after them or trying to convince them not to leave.

This advice may sound very "common sense" to someone rocking a healthy attachment style. But to an anxious attacher, preserving connections and preventing abandonment (even with deeply incompatible partners) can quite literally feel like a matter of life or death.

You will find so much freedom when you realize that the only way to relationship happiness is speaking up for yourself and your needs, and gracefully letting go of someone who isn't on board with that.
There are two possible outcomes here: if a potential partner runs away from you for speaking up, it makes you available to find someone who will embrace your needs. If, instead, that potential partner listens and has the desire

178

or ability to respond positively to your needs, then you'll become stronger and happier as a couple. Either outcome is *good*. The only option that isn't going to work out is sticking around and beating your head against a wall trying to force someone to honor your boundaries, needs, and love you in a way that they just can't seem to manage.

To be sure, this is easier said than done. But it's still an excellent thing to keep in mind when you're feeling fearful about opening up about your needs to a partner or romantic interest whom you're afraid will say no. It's important that we can learn to withstand hearing "no," respect their "no" without trying to change their mind, and then respect ourselves enough to ask "Is this going to be enough for me?" That's when we start turning away from partners who aren't a good fit and turn toward people who might be able to offer us the love we seek.

Another great tool for the anxious attacher in a fledgling relationship is to practice some *detachment*. Detachment means that you can separate your emotions, thoughts, wants, needs, and feelings from those belonging to other people. It's the idea that your partner's bad mood doesn't contaminate yours; you can still be happy (or at the very least, calm!) when they're in a funk. It means that you don't feel it's your personal mission to cheer them up every time they're down. It also means that you can keep the things that you want separate from the things that they want and maintain your identity as an individual. This concept may seem pretty basic, but, believe me, it's tougher than it sounds.

Living inside a mind that's screaming out for connection at all costs can make it very tough to separate your wants/needs from someone you feel that you need to connect to. Self-abandoning (giving up our identity, needs, and wants) can be second nature for Anxious Hearts. Even tougher, it's a toxic, repulsive behavior that pushes away the very people we seek to draw closer.

Detachment also means letting go of the need for things in your relationship to be a certain way.

Now, wait a minute! This doesn't mean that we settle for whatever we can get and blindly accept everything that comes our way. Not even close. Settling for sub-par relationships is not something I would *ever* advise. Rather, it is the idea that you can be happy no matter what other people do, up to and including "not being chosen by them." The way that you achieve this is by knowing that you've got your own back regardless of whether or not they choose you. In this more secure state, you will prefer being single over a relationship with someone who is not excited about you. It means that you don't waste your time trying to force behaviors that you desire and connections that just aren't there. It means you don't expend your energy trying to change or mold someone into your ideal partner. Ideally, you are a strong individual who has the fortitude to withstand the bad moods, behaviors, and undesirable characteristics of the people around you without trying to change/fix them, or having their shortcomings shake your happiness in any substantial way.

If only, right!?

It's not easy, but it *is* possible. Here are some tips to getting there:

- **Practice letting go of the need to control other people.** Remember that any change that you cause in someone will probably not be sustainable and only provide a temporary fix. People only really change and grow because *they want to* and put the work in themselves, not because someone else tells them to.

- **Learn how to make yourself happy.** Your happiness cannot be dictated by someone else. Take control of the ability to make yourself happy; know what you love and pursue it relentlessly, take care of yourself; build a life full of healthy relationships, and let romance be a bonus, not a requirement.

- **Practice mindfulness.** Learn to become more aware of your emotions and actions and try to notice them before you act on them. Curbing your automatic behaviors and taking a deeper look at why we do what we do (especially *before* we do it!) can save us a lot of heartache. Lastly, we must use that recognition to empower ourselves to take control of our own emotions and expectations.

When we find ourselves getting anxious about unmet needs or expectations, self-care is a good practice to turn to. We can use the feeling of "needing" something from someone else as a cue that we need to 1) communicate that need, but also 2) increase our focus on our own happiness and well-being. Exercise, meditation, or a creative outlet can help you redirect wasted nervous energy back toward yourself. It's important that we don't lose sight of these things when an exciting new partner steps into view.

It's easy to lose ourselves, our needs, and our independent happiness when wrapped up in all of the emotions of a shiny, new love interest. As an anxious attacher, especially, the temptation to hand over our happiness to someone else can be almost irresistible. They seem so capable!
So willing to step in where we fall short! And it's so much easier to hand over control than to deal with these difficult things yourself.

Don't give in to the urge to hand over your power, Anxious Heart. You're capable of so much more than you realize.

Find Relationship Role Models

You may have very little experience in a healthy relationship. Perhaps you have a hard time knowing what you want because you're not even sure what's reasonable to hope for or expect! This is common and happens for a myriad of reasons. Perhaps you're young and haven't been dating very long. Maybe you may have been married for years and now find yourself suddenly single. Many others grew up in environments where they weren't allow to have needs. Whatever the case, it can be hard to recognize what a healthy relationship looks like without the experience of one. We can adopt more secure beliefs and behaviors by finding secure relationship role models and observing their relationship.

Now, I'm not talking about Ross and Rachel, or Jim and Pam, or any other #RelationshipGoals fictitious couple that you wish you were part of. In fact, most of the couples from fiction should probably be avoided like the plague when you're looking for role models. This is because the kind of healthy relationship that you should aspire to would not make a very compelling story. Secure, healthy relationships contain a lot of consistency, mutual respect, trust, conflict resolution, and good communication. That doesn't make for a very exciting movie, does it?

Just to be clear, I'm not advocating for the pursuit of a boring love story. I want *much* more than that for you. I also want much more than that for myself!

What I'm saying is that the tension, drama, and toxic on-again, off-again will-they-or-won't-they suspense that make our favorite love stories so exciting typically come from an unhealthy place. The sagas of misunderstanding and struggle between two characters who have a *lot* of growing to do before they can live happily ever after make for some very exciting stories, but would produce tumultuous, miserable relationships in real life. So with that in mind, we're going to choose our relationship role models not based on their epic love stories, but instead, their stability and mutual respect.

Try to think of a couple you know whose relationship has withstood the test of time. Another great barometer of relationship health is if you have personally observed them treating each other with great respect. They may send out best friend vibes. The partnered friend or relative who you'd turn to for good advice would also be a great bet. Now that you've identified your role models, spend some time with them. What you're looking for here is behavior that you'd love to see in your own relationship. Take mental notes on what you see between them. You might notice that they include one another in conversation at a dinner party; one partner does not ignore or abandon the other. Maybe you chose your relationship role model because of the kind way that she always speaks about her partner—never critical and with a sweet sense of admiration.

I remember feeling struck by the care with which my role model couple treated each other. I knew right away that it was something I wanted for my own relationship. Another fascinating thing I observed was the way that they gave each other space when one was upset with the other. There was no fighting or relentless attempts to make negative feelings go away; they simply took time and space for themselves to calm down and recollect their thoughts and then brought the issue back up when they came back together calmly and knew what they wanted to say. Remarkable!

Look for ways that partners treat one another that you may not have known possible. You can then add the positive behaviors that you observe to your list of aspirations for your own current or future relationship. Write down what you see! Imagine yourself engaging in this healthy behavior with a future partner. Note how you feel when imagining this and indulge in this visualization often; it is a chance to rewire your brain toward more healthy relationship norms.

If you're able to talk to one of your role models, don't miss the chance to peek inside the inner workings of a secure attachment relationship. It can be such a treat listening to the ways that healthy couples discuss their partner and their relationship. The happiness and respect that they exude is contagious. And the wisdom that they dispense? Worth its weight in gold. Here are some suggestions on what to ask:

- What do you love most about your partner? Why?
- What do you think is the most important part of a healthy, happy relationship?
- What does it mean to be a good partner?
- What do you personally do to be a good partner in your relationship?

And remember, even the best relationships aren't all rainbows and sunshine. Make sure to ask your role model about the tougher parts of their relationship too. I find it particularly helpful to hear about the struggles that exist within the relationships that I most look up to. This gives me a fantastic perspective and reminds me that there's no such thing as the "perfect" relationship, even amongst the healthiest, happiest couples!

Here are some suggestions for asking about the darker side of relationships, if anyone is willing to reveal those nitty-gritty details:

- What kind of things do you two argue about?
  How do you solve them?
- What is hard for you in your relationship?
- How do you deal with it when your partner makes you feel sad/annoyed/angry?
- What do you think has gotten you through your toughest times as a couple?

Make sure to write down or journal these valuable pieces of advice.

Now that you've got some solid relationship goals written down, it's time to get serious about your study of secure attachers by identifying their traits.

Identifying Secure Attachers in the Wild

Ah, the coveted, elusive secure attacher. Gaze upon their posture of quiet confidence. See how they move smoothly through the dating pool avoiding drama, insecurity, and dodging poor matches with ease? So graceful! So effortless! So how do we make this happen for us?

Get your journal out again, Anxious Heart. The following are some serious #RelationshipGoals.

We need to be on the lookout for these splendid creatures on our dating adventures. We *also* need to know how to adopt this behavior into our own repertoire in order to attract and keep a secure attacher we find. So, without further ado, I present to you a bulleted list of secure attachment behaviors.

A securely attached person is:

- Confident without flattery or external validation. They *are not* cocky, arrogant, or conniving. Rather, they appear comfortable in their own skin and rock solid about their worth.
- Good at self-soothing. They probably don't require the input or help from lots of other people in order to feel good about themselves, their mood, their decisions, etc.
- Affected by other people's words, actions, or feelings but *not* defined by them and are able to regulate their own mental experience independently and healthily.
- Driven by love to help their partner feel better. They *are not* driven by fear or feel that it is their duty to fix/solve every problem their partner has, forsaking their own needs in the process.
- Able to healthily disagree or think differently than their partner. They *do not* seek to control what their partner thinks, feels, or does in order to make them feel more secure.
- Capable of feeling worthy and lovable on their own. They *do not* require a romantic partner to validate them first, or push away emotional validation/affection because they don't feel that it is deserved.
- Not going to waste time chasing, or avoiding. Secure attachers are comfortable being present with another person. They *don't* need excess validation or space to feel safe.

- A good communicator. They *do not* communicate their needs through passive aggressive remarks, sarcasm, pouting, acting out, attention seeking, whining, begging, or deceit.

- Open to intimacy and connection. They neither fear nor worship it. Rather, intimacy and connection feel nice for them. They will offer it and gladly accept it when it is offered. They will also refuse to self-abandon in order to get it.

You may be wondering where all these secures are hiding?

I've been on tons of dates. None of the people I meet are anything like this!

Statistically, this is unlikely. Secure attachers actually make up around 50% of the population. In a world of almost eight billion people, that means that a full four billion of them exhibit some, if not mostly secure traits. Although, I'll admit it's true that the older we get, the more insecure the dating pool becomes. To further depress you, it's another inconvenient truth that as the age of daters increases, the secure attachers get snapped up early and tend to stay in their relationships much, much longer than insecure attachers. As if I haven't already kicked you when you're down, secure and anxiously attached daters are extra-underrepresented in the dating pool; both groups tend to stay in their relationships longer than avoidants.

Remember back in Chapter 1 when we talked about insecure attachers needing insecurity in order to feel excited? Think of a date whom you may have labeled as "boring." Perhaps you later told a friend "there was just no spark." You either didn't call them back, sent a polite "thanks but no thanks" text, or worse, ghosted them.

I'm sorry to have to be the one to tell you, but there's a very real chance that this person was actually a secure attacher.
(There is a chance they were genuinely just boring, but hear me out!) It's an unfortunate cruel twist of fate about being an insecure attacher: secures can

feel boring to us. Here's why: insecure attachers are accustomed to anxiety, uncertainty, and drama in love. It is the turbulent, but familiar environment where we first learned about love. Those uncomfortable, unstable feelings are our "spark." Without our "spark," we quietly move on to the next person, unaware of the peace we'll be missing out on.

We want to make sure that we aren't missing out on great partners because of a lack of "spark." It's important to stay vigilant for healthy behaviors, even if they can feel a little dull. A secure attacher may require three or four dates before you really begin to feel a solid connection forming. It's one of the magical, sustainable things about a connection with someone who is secure. It takes some time to build, but once it's there, you can count on it being more real, durable, and stable.

So if you manage to find someone like this, how do you know if you're ready?

How Do You Know if You're Ready?

We've covered a lot of ground together! At this point, how would you evaluate your own readiness to date?

You may be getting conflicting messages on this topic from your parents, siblings, friends, or internet articles. Ultimately, it's up to you. No one else knows your unique circumstances, challenges, goals, or desires and you are the only one qualified to make that decision. I remember feeling 100% sure of my desire to get back into the dating pool, while simultaneously feeling completely clueless about whether or not that impulse was a good idea. I also remember feeling upset when friends and family told me not to; *who were they to decide!?*

The words of my therapist were a welcome, calm message among the storm of negativity and conflicting messages: "You are the only one who can decide whether or not you're ready to date." That's right! Your readiness to date is up to you and only you! You might (like I did) make a total mess of it because you don't have all the tools or confidence or know-how to make good dating decisions but ready or not, the decision whether or not to date is yours only, for better or worse.

For me, personally, the following points would have been helpful for me to know before I marched smugly into the battlefield and began left- and right-swiping. Feel free to use them to self-assess.

- Do you have massive anxiety regarding the outcome of a date? *This could mean that you may not be ready.*
- Do you worry about being judged as "good enough" by your date? *If so, you may not be ready.*
- Do you feel terror when imagining the end of a relationship? *If that's you, you may not be ready.*
- Does the idea of a partner treating you well make you extremely uncomfortable? *You guessed it, Anxious Heart. You may not be ready.*

And when I say that you may not be ready, what I mean is that you may want to start dating again, but without the tools to protect your heart or pick yourself back up, romance might be too stressful to be healthy for you right now. If this is the case, you *might* want to continue working on yourself and save the romantic dinners for later on.

Then again, dating can be nerve-racking for even the most confident daters! You may also be more adventurous than most! Alternately, here are points that may indicate dating-readiness...

- Do you believe you have your own back regardless of the date outcome? *You may be ready to date.*
- Do you have a wonderful support system (friends + family)? *You may be ready.*
- Do you have a very satisfying life without a relationship? *Go forth and date, my friend.*
- Are you ready and willing to give and receive intimacy and love and be vulnerable? *You may be ready to begin dating again.*

There are also some things that don't matter at all when considering your readiness to date!

- Are you in incredible shape? (The right partner won't care.)
- Have you fully healed all of your attachment struggles? (Psh. Almost no one has!)
- Has enough time elapsed between your previous relationship and your new dates? (There is no magical set amount of time to wait between relationships.)
- Do you live in a good city for dating? (Almost no city is any better for dating than any other one.)
- Is it the right season to be looking for love? (There's no correct time of year to date.)
- Will your ex be upset? (It doesn't matter what your ex thinks. This is about you.)

There are no definitive reasons to put off dating or to begin dating again. There are only *your* reasons and your feelings of readiness and they mean exactly what you think they do. It's tough to find people out there who say that they are "good at" dating or "enjoy it," so why put this kind of pressure on yourself? For the vast majority of us, dating is uncertain at best and mildly terrifying most of the other times. One thing is for certain: if you have confidence in yourself and know what you're looking for, you're going to have a much better time.

Identifying Red and Green Flags

Now, let's have a chat about flags.

Ask any dater what they're looking for, and most will rattle off a list of qualities that they seek in their ideal date: good looks, confidence, chemistry, charm. Others may list additional things like optimism, kindness, intelligence, similar life goals, and the like. These are all good and well. But as anxious attachers, there are some very important green flags and desirables that we should be in search of if we want a relationship to be a safe, enjoyable experience for us according to our unique relationship needs.

> **"You know, it's funny; when you look at someone through rose-colored glasses, all the red flags just look like flags."**
> **-Wanda, Bojack Horseman**

There are some traits that make a partner easier for an Anxious Heart to be with. These traits are our dating green flags which means when we spot them, we should proceed with the dating process. Forget dreamy eyes and a super-toned physique. Seek these traits that will help soothe the warning bells before they even have the chance to sound.

Comfort communicating
Emotional availability (vulnerable, affectionate)
Enjoys spending time with their significant other
Enjoys giving and receiving affection

Highly stable (less volatile emotions)
Open, honest, and trusting
Empathetic and caring

These traits are precisely the kind of things that prevent and soothe relationship anxiety caused by anxious attachment. Daters are often focused on superficial traits when looking for a significant other. Physical beauty, charm, artistic or athletic talent, and income are all very appealing and can be fun when we find them in an exciting new partner. But these surface level traits do nothing to calm us when things get rough. And in *every* relationship, things are going to get rough every now and then.

In a particularly memorable conversation with my therapist, he asked me what kind of traits I was looking for as I navigated the dating world. Of course, I started talking about shared interests, physical attraction, confidence, and other common desires. His advice was not something I'd ever considered before.

"What if, instead of having a checklist of must-have traits, you made a list of deal breakers and then just stayed open to whatever good things a date had to offer?" He specified that the deal breaker list should consist only of things that would be legitimate deal breakers for me (i.e. abuse, criticism, emotional unavailability, someone openly not wanting the same kind of relationship that I do...) His suggestion was a revelation. In fact, this strategy would crack the dating pool wide open for me. Following his advice, I found myself regularly on dates with men whom I would not normally have given a chance before, enjoying many unexpected and unfamiliar qualities that I found I really enjoyed. It was such a different dating experience than I was used to!

In the past, my search for "confidence" had brought me face-to-face with a lot of arrogance. Requiring very good looks had put me across the table from more than a few shallow, beautiful guys who weren't seeking much more than physical beauty themselves. An amazing sense of humor was sometimes a mask for an inability to talk about serious issues. Men who were mysterious and aloof were appealing but also triggered every attachment anxiety inside me.

But after following my therapist's advice, I was finding myself on very different kinds of dates. When I opened myself up to new possibilities, I met men who were extraordinarily responsible and stable. I was meeting men who were thoughtful and kind. I met excellent communicators who did not shy away from tough topics. There were intellectuals, empaths, and men possessing incredible thoughtfulness!

The experiment really drove home the idea that the green flags I sought out before were not the way to happiness. I had to throw out the flags labeled "tall," "charming," and "witty." It was clear that they needed to be replaced with flags labeled "communicative," "affectionate," and "honest."

Again, I'm not saying you should throw out your hopes and dreams for an attractive, charming partner. This isn't about giving up on finding physical attraction or impressive wit. It simply means that you might consider opening your door a little bit wider and having an open mind about the kinds of things that can turn you on to someone new. The best partner for you might not be tall; but they could be thoughtful. They might not have perfect teeth; but they very well might have perfect timing when you need a kind word. They may not make an impressive income; but they might love their job so much that they radiate energy even on the weekends.

And while you're out there exploring, keep your heart and mind open and take off those rose-tinted glasses for a moment. Red flags are our "no-go" traits. Some red flags are obvious. Physical or mental abuse, severe personality/mental disorders, addictions, emotional unavailability, or a big difference in values are going to make dating someone a real struggle.

It's usually easier to see the big, obvious red flags and steer clear. But there are some traits that anxious attachers don't typically see as negative. Even worse, some of those traits can feel downright appealing. These traits tend to rub against our sore spots in ways that hearken back to the pain of our childhood. It's a pain that, when unexamined and unaddressed, we tend to lean toward and tragically misinterpret as "passion" or "a spark."

This isn't because we're glutton for punishment, but rather, the problem traits that Anxious Hearts find themselves drawn to again and again in relationships are appealing because they are *familiar*. And familiarity, even when unpleasant, can be more comfortable than uncertainty. Our dynamic with someone who has those problematic traits (distance, emotional unavailability, etc.) may mirror unmet needs that we experienced as children. This pattern of relating then reminds us of the ways that we experienced love when life was new and our brains were still learning how the world worked.

Do you remember the child in the Strange Situation Test? A child who felt wounded by their mother's neglect may feel abandoned by a partner but they *also* may feel a comforting familiarity in the distance.

This is familiar. When I love someone, they are too busy for me. This is how love has always felt for me. This must be love.

The brain, even as it ages, remembers feeling unsure and worried and abandoned. And even though that worry hurts, it's familiar. It is maybe all that we know of "love." Often, as adults whose anxious attachment is very long-standing, we don't even know what to do with prospective partners who are consistently available and reassuring. Maybe we've never experienced someone who was very reassuring before! Their availability then doesn't feel like love as we know it. It feels undeserved. Sometimes it can even feel fake.

Once we become aware of anxious attachment in ourselves, it's vital that we protect our hearts from repeating the damaging patterns from childhood. We can consciously choose to walk away from partners who exhibit traits that feel like "home" but cause us so much pain.

The following traits would be red flags for anyone but are especially harmful for anxious attachers.

- Needs an excessive amount of space/alone time
- Uncomfortable with affection
- Critical
- Very private and/or uncomfortable discussing personal matters and emotions
- Projects unavailability (married/uninterested in a serious or exclusive relationship)
- Highly emotional/impulsive/moody

It's not enough to simply identify green and red flags. We must accept that we're worthy of love, want healthy love for ourselves, and practice seeking and accepting healthy love and attention.

But how do I do that!? I'm not even sure what healthy love looks like, let alone have any way to practice accepting it.

Don't worry, I've got you, Anxious Heart.

How to Practice and Accept Healthy Love

How can you possibly learn to behave in healthy, loving ways without first finding a healthy partner who doesn't mind joining you on your journey through anxiety and insecurity? It can feel like an impossible wish. One is reminded of the saying, "You can't get a job without experience, and you can't get experience without a job." But I have great news, Anxious Hearts: there are actually *many* ways to learn and practice healthy love before you get into the relationship of your dreams!

The very best thing you can do to move yourself toward secure attachment is to grab a close friend or even your relationship role model, and ask them if they'll help you. Explain some of the relationship behaviors you struggle with (for example, stating your needs, a difficulty trusting, fearing abandonment, being overly sensitive or highly emotional, etc.) and ask them if they will help you work on these when they see them happening. Chances are they'll be delighted to aid you on your journey.

Having someone as a secure anchor helps you build trust with others, even if this person is not a romantic attachment for you. For example, if you find it very difficult to speak up about your needs or say no, positive experiences with your friend or role model will help you practice these skills and also teach you that it can be safe to ask for what you need or say no when you need to.

At the beginning of a budding relationship, if the person you're dating has proven through their behavior that they're safe to be vulnerable with,

196

you can also ask them if they'll help you work on these healthy relationship behaviors. They may even have similar issues of their own that they'd like your help with. It can be incredibly bonding to help each other heal and bring these kinds of issues up early so that you can work on them before they become problematic. It can also help you in becoming very clear about the kind of communication and secure attachment goals that you aspire to.

Grab your journal or a piece of paper. You're going to write down a list full of traits that you're working on. Sometimes it can help to think of the person who you want to be. Start with the most important few things. Read these every single day before bed or when you start your day. And I'm not saying that you're going to nail it at first, or even soon, but if you create a list of behaviors and mindsets to aspire to and you read it every day, little by little you will notice changes.

Take the first few items that you've identified as being very important to you and put them in a highly visible place. Some examples:

Place a sticky note on your mirror:
"I will speak up when something bothers me."

Write it on your hand:
"I take deep breaths before reacting to something upsetting."

Tape a sign to your refrigerator:
"I prioritize the hobbies, interests, and things that make me ME."

Healthy Love in a New Relationship

So you've been working on noticing healthy love and behaving in secure ways. After a date or two (or three or four…) you find yourself in a budding relationship or on the cusp of something that could turn into one. It's exciting and not just a little bit scary. *Am I ready? How do I know this one will be different?* Well, the good news is that all relationships are different, so that one is a guarantee. With a more solid foundation under your feet, hopefully you'll be coming into this one a more resilient, well-rounded, and confident person, full of concrete ideas about what you want and some new communication tools to get you there. No matter how much growth and confidence you're now enjoying, take caution! You must keep in mind that an anxious attacher has the unfortunate habit of speeding toward intimacy and commitment, and a new (or false!) sense of confidence and self-assuredness can make this tendency even worse.

Slow your roll, Anxious Heart.

You may be feeling like a rock star but it's vital that now, at your most confident, you don't throw yourself prematurely into a relationship with someone who feels good but hasn't proved their mettle.

Clinical counselor John Van Epp wrote a wonderful book on the subject of developing healthy new relationships called How to Avoid Falling in Love with a Jerk.[24] Central to the book is an idea he developed called the "Relationship Attachment Model," or the RAM. You're going to want to keep this model in your back pocket if you're considering getting romanti-

---

24 Van Epp, J. (2008). How to Avoid Falling in Love with a Jerk: The Foolproof Way To Follow Your Heart Without Losing Your Mind (1st ed.). New York: McGraw-Hill Education. Northfield Publishing.

cally close to someone new. This bad boy is going to save you some serious grief if you can follow it closely.

Dr. Van Epp asks us to imagine a sound system's equalizer. Each slider represents an aspect of our relationship with someone that we can turn the volume up or down on. The equalizer knobs are labeled from left to right:

Know, Trust, Rely, Commit, Touch.

Anxious folks will often barrel into relationships headfirst and without any thought. They foolishly start at the right side of the equalizer and make their way slowly left. Touch, often the easiest, but most dangerous way of getting to know someone (especially for the anxiously attached!) is cranked up to eleven right off the bat. Sexual tension, flirting, and even sex often precedes our efforts to get to know or commit to someone. We fall into patterns of dysfunction and hooking-up with judgment clouded by a heavy fog of pheromones and sex-fueled dopamine. We may commit because the sexual connection is great. Then comes the gradual process of learning to rely on them and, lastly, (if we're lucky) a deep trust and intimate knowing starts to develop weeks, months, or even years after a couple first hooks up.

Dr. Epp wisely suggests that we should do just the opposite. Ditch the pheromone cloud and start turning those dials up from the left to the right, instead. Here it is again: Know, Trust, Rely, Commit, Touch.

His method is particularly useful for anxious attachers who tend to dive into a relationship, desperately building connection before the relationship has proved to be a safe place to do that. If we can make ourselves start with the knowing (facilitated by lots of talking, observing how they act around friends, and family, and us), it can naturally develop into an evidence-based trust. We come to know them and see from their behavior that they are trustworthy. From here, we can find ourselves coming to rely on someone who has shown us their good character and dependability. Commitment comes much easier after all of this proof we've seen, and by the time a couple gets to the touch, they can really enjoy it, knowing that the person they're getting physically intimate with is a wonderful and safe choice for them.

If you can keep the RAM in mind the next time you're getting to know someone, you may find the entire process a *lot* less daunting. This can allow us to show up as our real, vulnerable selves and experience real, healing intimacy within a relationship.

Boundaries in a New Relationship

So how do you show up as your real, vulnerable self without feeling the terror of rejection or getting hopelessly walked on? We touched on boundaries in Chapter 4, but they're definitely worth exploring more on your own beyond this book. Boundaries are the safety net that allow you to show up as your genuine self without worrying about being taken advantage of. If you're not sure whether or not you'll uphold your values or needs in the face of someone else's desires, you may tend to withdraw into yourself rather than staying open. But when you feel safe, knowing that you've got your own back and can uphold healthy boundaries for yourself, you'll be freer to show up in a genuine way and love someone out loud.

Boundaries can be scary, especially if you're not used to setting them! If you're unfamiliar with the concept of boundary setting, you might worry that setting a boundary is "mean," or will push your partner or love interest away. In truth, boundaries are kind, healthy, and bring people *closer* to you. Knowing that you're being authentic and not people pleasing allows others to know you fully...*the real you*. It allows trust to build between two people.

It feels important to take this moment to distinguish between a boundary and an ultimatum. An ultimatum seeks to control someone else's actions. It says: "If you don't do this, I won't do that." A boundary only seeks to control our own actions. *I cannot allow myself to engage in this behavior with you because this doesn't align with my values.* Boundaries show compassion for, commitment to, and control over our own emotions and actions. They also help us protect ourselves from the actions of others that hurt or drain us.

Relationships are only as scary as the boundaries you allow them to break.

That said, boundaries can be tough for the anxiously attached. But in spite of their difficulty, they're a prerequisite for a healthy, happy relationship with anyone (even *yourself*)!

Here's the quick rundown on how to implement boundaries:

Get familiar with the feeling that your boundaries have been violated.

This could feel like a punch in the gut, or a creeping sense of dread or regret. Start noticing the feeling that you're over-giving, unhappy, have been shorted, that you are unappreciated, or are feeling drained. These are some signs your boundaries may have been crossed.

Be assertive when you recognize that a boundary has been violated.

Let someone know that they have violated your boundary, and stand tall in your willingness to defend and protect the boundaries you set for yourself.

Forgive yourself if you fail, and keep trying.

Learning to set boundaries is hard. You're probably not going to get it right the first time, and you're not going to be good at it without loads of practice.

Be willing to let someone go who doesn't respect your boundaries.

It's much harder to learn and enforce healthy boundaries when a relationship is established. It can be much easier to set expectations early on so that your boundaries are not negotiable or weak.

Relationships are only as scary as the boundaries you allow them to break. But with healthy boundaries in place, you're free to get straight to the good part of a new relationship—giving and receiving love.

The Negativity Bias

Anxious attachers are usually much more focused on looking for signs that we're being hurt or abandoned than we are on appreciating the ways that we're being loved. A person's own negativity bias is partly to blame here. It's not a terrible thing, and it actually makes a lot of sense: when our brains were developing back in our cave days, it was wise for people to pay more attention to which berries made us sick; after all, it could be a matter of life or death! But the propensity for focusing on the negative and ignoring the good in our relationships is on hyper-drive for an Anxious Heart. We can enjoy an entire day of happiness with our partners and find our evening completely derailed by a comment that rubs us the wrong way. This is our negativity bias in action.

One excellent way to combat negativity bias is to redirect our focus on the good. Pay attention to the ways that someone shows you love. Write it down! To help fight my own negativity bias in relationships, I have a journal where I make a note every single day of all the sweet/kind/loving things that my partner did for me during the day. I do not write the things that bugged or hurt me in that journal. And when I'm feeling particularly nervous, unloved, or even abandoned, I turn to my log of sweet actions, words, and gestures. Reminding myself of my partner's kindness has saved me many uncomfortable phone calls or resorting to destructive protest behaviors in an attempt to reconnect.

I have also created the Anxious Hearts Gratitude Journal (available on AnxiousHeartsGuide.com or on Amazon.) It is specifically designed to help anxious attachers take note of the positives within their relationship so that they can combat their negativity bias.

Learning to overcome our negativity bias and focus on the ways that our partners are caring for us is an important step in learning to accept and receive healthy love. When we make efforts to notice and appreciate acts of love directed toward us, we can calm our own warning bells before the alarm goes off.

No gesture or effort is too small! Some carry significantly more meaning than they appear to. Does your partner do little things often to make sure you're comfortable? Do they anticipate your needs? Do they go out of their way for you, fix things around your house, or put time and effort into cooking special meals that they know you will enjoy?

Anxious Hearts are often desperate to hear "I love you," and yet we can be tragically tone-deaf when it comes to hearing our partners shouting their love with their time, attention, or loving acts of service.

Instead of laser focusing on what they *aren't doing for you*, try to pay close attention to ways that they affirm the relationship and connection. Keep in mind your propensity toward ignoring the good and seeking out confirmation that they are abandoning you. This is yet another example of your anxiety lying to you. Secure attachers are especially good at soaking up the good and letting the annoying, small stuff roll off their backs (or healthily addressing problems as they arise).

When we can find a good partner, take things at a thoughtful, healthy pace, exercise healthy boundaries, and redirect our focus to highlight the love they show us—amazing things can happen for us. In environments like this, we may find our relationship anxieties melting away. When we are consistently met with empathy, understanding, and validation, it frees us up to do our own inner healing work. It doesn't get much more secure than that. Imagine how much you could accomplish and what you could do for yourself if you weren't pouring all of your energy into trying to be understood, feeling heard, and feeling confident that you're loved.

The idea that a relationship can make us better and stronger (rather than constantly stress us out) is what all this healing is about. A relationship shouldn't be a place of mostly struggle and stress. With the tools we've covered together, I hope you're excited about what your relationship could be—a great source of joy and an avenue for growth.

If you can push through the discomfort of your anxious attachment, the work won't be easy, but there is beautiful healing waiting for you on the other side.

Homework/Reading Assignments

Here are your *last* reading assignments. You've come so far...don't stop now!

These last books are relationship-enhancers. They were chosen to level you up within a relationship that's worth enhancing. Our ability to recognize, give, and receive love is vital to our enjoyment of the relationship, and there's a little something in each one of these that will make you a little bit (or a lot!) better as a partner. Knowing ourselves deeply and understanding our tendencies during our search for love can help us avoid the pitfalls that have ruined our efforts in the past.

The 5 Love Languages *by Gary Chapman*[25]

It's critical that you know how to recognize the way that you (and the people you love) best express and receive affection. This knowledge alone can make our romantic relationships so much more fulfilling. The author offers free quizzes on his website 5LoveLanguages.com. Additionally, the internet abounds with articles about each of the love languages and how to become more fluent in any one of them. I don't know a single person who has read this book who hasn't benefited from an increased capacity to show love and recognize love being shown to them.

How To Avoid Falling in Love with a Jerk *by John Van Epp*[26]

Remember the "RAM" (Relationship Attachment Model)? This is where it was born! I picked his book up on a whim. I wasn't prepared for the level of wisdom I found inside.

---

25 Chapman, G. (2014). The 5 Love Languages: The Secret to Love that Lasts. Chicago: Moody Publishers.
26 Van Epp, J. (2008). How to Avoid Falling in Love with a Jerk: The Foolproof Way To Follow Your Heart Without Losing Your Mind (1st ed.). New York: McGraw-Hill Education. Northfield Publishing.
.

Dr. Epp's book was well-researched and packed full of amazing, practical dating advice. The author presented a different way of looking at chemistry and compatibility that I'd never considered before. The idea of increasing closeness in earned levels really changed my dating game for the better.

If you're currently in a relationship, don't skip these books. The 5 Love Languages isn't about finding someone who expresses affection in the exact same way you do; it's about understanding the different ways that people give/receive affection. And Dr. Van Epp's book, although geared toward daters, taught me concepts that I used to improve my current relationship.

Whether partnered or searching, there's always room to improve our communication, become more aware of the ways that we're showing up in relationships, and gain a deeper understanding of relationship dynamics.

"THE FIRST STEP TOWARDS GETTING SOMEWHERE IS TO DECIDE YOU'RE NOT GOING TO STAY WHERE YOU ARE."

J.P. MORGAN

CONCLUSION

I believe in you, Anxious Heart.

Searching for the kind of big love that people dream about is stressful—even secure folks report having an awful time of it. But when you add an insecure, overactive attachment system on top of that, it can make finding love or personal happiness feel impossible.

You can move your attachment style closer to secure. I believe in you because I know that it's not just possible, it's very doable. I have experienced the change firsthand. When I started this journey, I was as anxiously attached as they come. In what now feels like a past life, I spent entire evenings ruminating about the ways that my needs were not being met. I was a people pleaser as my default mode. I convinced myself that I had no needs and that I enjoyed endlessly and enthusiastically serving everyone else. My anxiety and dissatisfaction grew daily. The world seemed like a bleak, hopeless place where I was doomed to forever run on a treadmill of other people's wants and needs, never finding my own happiness or joy in relationships.

Socially, I hung by a thread, terrified of doing anything that might displease the people I love for fear that their love/attention might slip through my hands.

When I discovered through my reading that there could be a different way, I knew I didn't want the kind of life I had been living. And I don't want it for you. The work to get to the other side is challenging but absolutely not impossible. I dove into the work with my whole heart, as I hope that you will do.

It may feel like you're scaling a mountain right now. The work in front of you is unfamiliar, arduous, and intimidating like none other. But a good friend told me once that climbing a mountain is much easier when you focus on taking smaller steps. And, of course, just keep plugging away until you can see the top.

With this tactic in mind, I have been trudging up my own personal mountain for years, implementing the secure techniques I have learned, relentlessly pursuing my passions, and building my support system with friends and family that I can lean on when things get tough. Little by little, both inside and outside of romantic relationships, I have felt my relationship anxiety melting away. I have enjoyed a new confidence, self-love, and more happiness in my relationships. Honestly, the work has led to a better sense of well-being overall. From that place of increased well-being, I knew I wanted to share that information with others who need it. In creating The Anxious Hearts Guide on Instagram, I found a community of thousands of other anxious attachers who were also hard at work on healing their attachment struggles. I also found other professionals who were passionate about spreading this message. Every comment and message has helped me with my own healing. I am grateful beyond words. I know that I couldn't have written this book without the help of my fellow Anxious Hearts.

You, the Anxious Heart who holds these words in your hands, are the reason for this project, and I want to thank you for coming on this journey with me. If you are able to take just one idea or piece of advice, gain a better understanding about how your mind works, or develop a single new habit/perspective from your reading here, I will consider this project a wild success. Hopefully, you take away several!

If you're not an Anxious Heart, and are simply reading this to better understand an anxious attacher you care about, I also want to thank you. For them, but also on behalf of all of us. We can be a nervous, overthinking, sensitive crowd who often feel overlooked and misunderstood. It can be incredibly tough for us to speak up about what we need. Your interest in our hearts and minds *really does* mean the world to us.

Maya Angelou said, "Do the best you can until you know better. Then when you know better, do better."

You know better now, my friend. You're not going to be planning your wedding as soon as you swipe right. You're not going to overshare the moment you get an opening in the conversation. Hopefully, you won't start sweating anymore over a five-minute-old unanswered text. If you've done your work here, I hope that you can stop wishing someone would love you before they've even given you a good reason to want their affection. It is my hope that you'll know that you are worthy of the love you seek, and you can act and think accordingly.

And don't be too hard on yourself because simply knowing isn't enough. This stuff takes *so* much practice to master. Healing comes from the diligent practice of independence, self-love, and assertive communication that you've been lacking all these years. And little by little, as you practice and these things build up within you, you will find that life and love isn't so complicated after all. Sometimes it can even be kind of...wonderful.

I hope that you can stop labeling the things in your romantic life as good or bad, and start asking yourself, "Is this working for me?" I hope that you can stop punishing yourself for doing things "wrong" and instead start supporting yourself in the daily practice of becoming who you want to be. You're going to have missteps. You may even regularly screw things up again before you start getting it right. But when the voice in your head stops berating you, you won't be as comfortable with taking that tone from other people, either. When the voice in your head starts sounding a lot more forgiving and accepting, even loving, you're going to start finding love all around you.

Because the fact of the matter, Anxious Heart, is that you don't need to be perfect to be loved.

My hope is that you will learn to derive your happiness and worthiness from your own active pursuit and focus of the things that you love; the things that make you you. This includes your own human missteps and fumbles as well. The right person will love you not "in spite of your struggles," but rather "with them." You won't need to be perfect or "fixed" to receive their love. They'll see the whole messy package, size it up, and say, "Yep. I'm in." And they'll support, admire, and appreciate the work that you're putting in to overcome your struggles.

And while you don't need to be perfect or 100% healed to find love, you do have to be ready for it. This means that you're doing the work, you are responsible for your own feelings, and are excited to fully show up for someone as the best *you* that you can be. You're working at not giving in to activating strategies and protest behavior. Either insecure behavior is at a minimum or you're actively working on recognizing and squashing it as it arises. You're communicating about your needs and putting effort in every day to overcome the things that aren't working for you. And last, trust that there *are* people out there with big love to give you. If you exist with

> **Strength doesn't come from what you can do. It comes from overcoming the things you once thought you couldn't.**
>
> **- Rikki Cloos**

all the love that you have to give, it stands to reason that there *must* be others. If we stop trying to give our love to those who are resistant and instead focus on what we truly want, we will find others who are ready, willing, and excited to embark with us on the kind of love story that people dream about.

Lastly, you're far from alone. Thousands upon thousands of people are also on self-improvement journeys like this. Some of them probably live near you. Some of them are even sexy and fun! Some of them would be thrilled to meet you, in all your weird, wonderful, flawed-but-fabulous glory. Talk to others about your goals. Find people who support your growth and want to grow with you. You may also find yourself inspiring the people around you when your growth starts to become too big and obvious to ignore.

Strength doesn't come from what you can do. No strong person likely started out that way. Strength comes from overcoming the things you once thought you couldn't—the things that feel too big to rise above—but little by little, you will find yourself growing and achieving beyond your wildest hopes and dreams. If this all sounds a little starry-eyed and too-good-to-be-true, I understand. It's just that I've experienced this growth and at its best, it's nothing short of magic. Through the tears and confusion, self-help books and scribbled journal pages, heart-wrenching therapy sessions and awkward communication blunders there really is something wonderful on the other side of all that work and pain. It's not perfect self-esteem or a perfect partner, either. (Mostly because those things don't exist!) But when you can understand your struggles, accept the flaws in yourself and others, acknowledge your needs and forgive yourself for having them, and learn to communicate in ways that honor everyone's struggles and needs, the world becomes your oyster.

When you create the kind of life for yourself that helps you meet many of your own needs, you simply *require less* of your partner. This creates an environment where they're freer to approach and love you in the ways they can. You both begin to enjoy each other more, feeling less pressure to be any certain way. This is the space where secure attachment and healthy relationships are born. It's the place where you stop asking, *"What can I do to be enough for them?"* And instead affirm, *"I am good at making myself happy. Does this person add to my happiness? If so, how can I make them happy in return?"*

It's a life where the massive energy you used to devote to making others approve of you is redirected toward your passions and loving yourself. It's more time for the friends who truly care, more bandwidth for hobbies and passion projects. It's a life that's more *you* than the one you're living now.

And you know who's going to fall head over heels for the genuine version of you that no one has ever seen before? Well, *you*, of course. And as a bonus, other people will also find that pretty darn sexy as well.

So, here we are, Anxious Heart. Your glorious, bright future. My hope is that you feel different than you did when you first started reading—more capable, more hopeful, more *you*. You may be at the very beginning of your journey or somewhere closer to the middle. Wherever you are, I believe in this work and in your ability to change your mind and your experience of love.

If you've got the drive to change your attachment style and embrace the tools and methods for change, I believe in a future for all Anxious Hearts with significantly less anxiety and significantly more of the kind of love that's always felt just out of your grasp.

SOCIAL MEDIA ACCOUNTS

FOR INSECURE ATTACHERS

@anxiousheartsguide

@dating.intentionally

@drelizabethfedrick

@drstantatkin

@elizabeth.gillette

@fixyourpicker

@gottmaninstitute

@haileypaigemagee

@h.e.l.e.n.m.a.r.i.e

@heydrjustine

@jason.vanruler

@jillianturecki

@jimmy_on_relationships

@lizlistens

@millennial.therapist

@mindfulmft

@rebeccaorecoaching

@terricole

@theanxietyhealer

@theartofhealingbytrevor

@Theempoweredtherapist

@TheEQSchool

@theinneryats

@thejessicadasilva

@therapyjeff

@thelovedrive

@TheLovingAvoidant

@thematthewhussey

@TheSecureRelationship

@your.being

@your.relationship.reset

RECOMMENDED BOOKS
FOR INSECURE ATTACHERS

Attached *by Rachel Heller and Amir Levine*

Anxiously Attached: Becoming More Secure in Life and Love *by Jessica Baum*

Attachment Theory Workbook for Couples *by Elizabeth Gillette*

The Better Boundaries Workbook *by Sharon Martin, MSW, LCSW*

The Chemistry Between Us: Love, Sex, and the Science of Attraction
by Larry Young, PhD and Brian Alexander

**The Origins of You: How Breaking Family Patterns
Can Liberate the Way We Live and Love** *by Vienna Pharaon*

Big Dating Energy *by Jeff Guenther and Kate Happ*

**Boundary Boss: The Essential Guide to
Talk True, Be Seen, and (Finally) Live Free** *by Terri Cole*

Codependent No More *by Melody Beattie*

Difficult Conversations: How to Discuss What Matters Most *by Bruce Patton*

**Facing Love Addiction: Giving Yourself the Power to
Change the Way You Love** *by Pia Mellody*

Getting Past Your Breakup *by Susan J. Elliott*

Hold Me Tight: Seven Conversations for a Lifetime of Love
by Dr. Sue Johnson

How to Be an Adult in Relationships: The Five Keys to Mindful Loving
by David Richo

I Hear You: The Surprisingly Simple Skill Behind Extraordinary Relationships
by Michael S. Sorensen

**Insecure in Love: How Anxious Attachment Can Make You Feel Jealous, Needy,
and Worried and What You Can Do About It** *by Leslie Becker-Phelps PhD*

Nonviolent Communication: A Language of Life *by Marshall Rosenberg*

Secure Love: Create a Relationship That Lasts *by Julie Menanno*

Set Boundaries, Find Peace: A Guide to Reclaiming Yourself
by Nedra Glover Tawwab

Stop People Pleasing: And Find Your Power *by Hailey Magee*

The Highly Sensitive Person in Love *by Elaine N. Aron, PhD*

The Power of Attachment *by Diane Poole Heller, PhD*

Wired for Love *by Stan Tatkin, PsyD*

ABOUT THE AUTHOR

Rikki Cloos is the writer and creator behind the Instagram account @AnxiousHeartsGuide, where a half million 'Anxious Hearts' find information and relational healing. A raging bibliophile and recovering 'anxious heart' herself, she holds degrees in Creative Nonfiction Writing, Communications Studies, and Graphic Design. Her divorce, deep dive into attachment theory, and involvement with the self-help community online inspired her to write the book that she would have needed years ago; approachable, accessible, and enlightening; a window into why we do the frustrating things that we do for love - and how to rise above it. When she isn't writing, she's either indoors reading about relationships or outside adventuring in beautiful Anchorage, Alaska.

A review on Amazon is the best way to help other anxious attachers find this book! If you've got any concerns or feedback that would negatively affect your review, I ask that you send me a message on Instagram and allow me to address it personally; your feedback can positively affect future print and digital editions of The Anxious Hearts Guide.

For more information on anxious attachment, follow @AnxiousHeartsGuide on Instagram, visit the Anxious Hearts Guide website (www.AnxiousHeartsGuide.com) or search for 'Rikki Cloos' on Amazon or Audible.